CONTINENTS IN CLOSE-UP

NORTH AMERICA

MALCOLM PORTER and KEITH LYE

RAINTREE
STECK-VAUGHN
PUBLISHERS

Copyright © Malcolm Porter and AS
Publishing (1999)

First published 1999
by Cherrytree Press Limited

First published in the United States 2002
by Raintree Steck-Vaughn Publishers

Library of Congress Cataloging in
Publication Data,

Porter, Malcolm
    North America. - (continents in close-up)
    1.Children's atlases
    2.North America - Maps for children
    I.Title II.Lye, Keith
    912.7

ISBN 0 7398 3238 7

Printed in Hong Kong

CONTINENTS IN CLOSE-UP
NORTH AMERICA

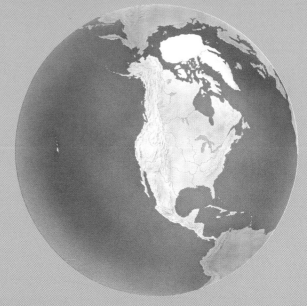

This illustrated atlas combines maps, pictures, flags, globes,
information panels, diagrams, and charts to give an overview
of the whole continent and a closer look at each of its countries.

COUNTRY CLOSE-UPS

Each double-page spread has these
features:

Introduction The author introduces the
most important facts about the country
or region.

Globes A globe on which you can see the
country's position on the continent and in
the world.

Flags Every country's flag is shown.

Information panels Every country has an
information panel that gives its area,
population, and capital, and where
possible its currency, religions, languages,
main cities, and government.

Pictures Captioned illustrations of
important features give a flavor of the
country. You can find out about physical
features, famous people, ordinary people,
animals, plants, places, products, and
much more.

Maps Every country is shown on a
clear, accurate map. To get the most out
of the maps it helps to know the symbols,
which are shown in the key on the
opposite page.

Land You can see by the coloring on
the map where the land is forested,
frozen, or desert.

Height Relief hill shading shows the
location of mountain ranges. Individual
mountains are marked by a triangle.

Direction All of the maps are drawn
with north at the top of the page.

Scale All of the maps are drawn to scale
so that you can find the distance
betweeen places in miles or kilometers.

0	200 miles
0	200 kilometers

KEY TO MAPS

CANADA	Country name
TEXAS	Province or state name
~~	Country border
■	More than 1 million people*
●	More than 500,000 people
•	Less than 500,000 people
☐	Country capital
★	State or province capital
ROCKY MTS	Mountain range
▲ Mt McKinley 20,440 ft (6,194 m)	Mountain with its height
∴ Tikal	Archaeological site

Ohio	River
	Canal
	Lake
	Dam
	Island

	Forest
	Crops
	Dry grassland
	Desert
	Tundra
	Polar

Many large cities, such as Boston, have metropolitan populations that are greater than the city figures. Such cities have larger dot sizes to emphasize their importance.

CONTINENT CLOSE-UPS

People and Beliefs Map of population densities; chart of percentage of population per country; chart of areas of countries; map of religions; chart of main religious groups.

Climate and Vegetation Map of vegetation from polar to desert; map of winter and summer temperatures; map of annual rainfall; diagram of mountain climates.

Ecology and Environment Map of environmental problems and disasters; map of earthquake zones, volcanoes, hurricanes and tornadoes; diagram of greenhouse effect; panel of endangered animals and plants.

Economy Map of agricultural and industrial products; chart of gross national products for individual countries; panel on per capita gross national products; map of sources of energy.

Politics and History Map of political systems; panel of great events; timeline of important dates; panel showing Viking longship and Voyager space probe; map of location of major events in North American history.

———

Index All the names on the maps and in the picture captions can be found in the index at the end of the book.

CONTENTS

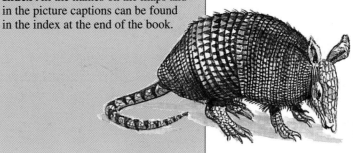

Armadillo
see page 18

NORTH AMERICA

North America is the third-largest continent, after Asia and Africa. The two biggest countries, Canada and the United States, are among the world's richest. These two high-income countries have many high-tech industries, and most people there enjoy comfortable lives. Mexico and the countries of Central America and the Caribbean are low- or middle-income countries. Many of their people are poor.

The climate of North America varies greatly from north to south. A huge ice sheet covers most of Greenland in the northeast, with smaller ice caps in northern Canada. The southern parts of North America lie in the hot and humid tropics.

ALASKA (US)

PACIFIC OCEAN

Whales swim off the west coast of North America, and people enjoy watching them. Many North Americans believe that the development of the land and sea should be controlled so that wildlife and natural wonders can be conserved.

Golden Gate Bridge in San Francisco, California, is one of North America's most famous landmarks. San Francisco was rebuilt after a great earthquake in 1906. Earthquakes and volcanic eruptions occur in western North America and in the Caribbean.

Market days, where farmers sell their produce and buy goods for their families, are important events in Central America. Farming employs more than 30 percent of the people of tropical North America. Many farmers are poor and struggle to survive.

Combine harvesters are used on the huge grain farms of Canada and the United States. Farming is highly mechanized there and employs only three percent of the people. The farms are, however, much more productive than those in the countries to the south.

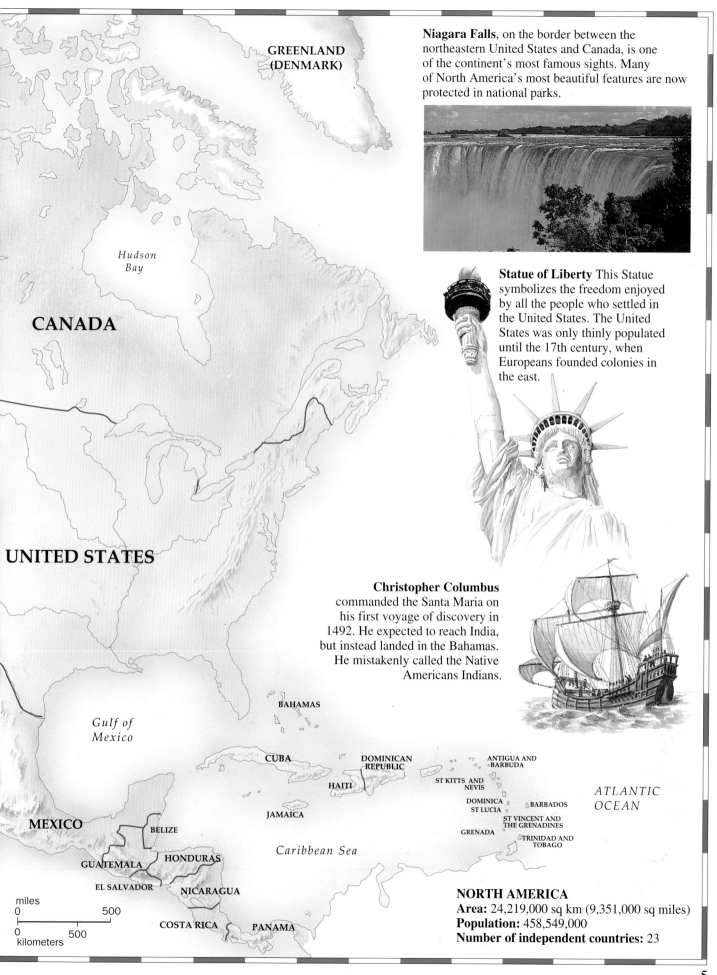

GREENLAND
(DENMARK)

Niagara Falls, on the border between the northeastern United States and Canada, is one of the continent's most famous sights. Many of North America's most beautiful features are now protected in national parks.

Hudson Bay

CANADA

Statue of Liberty This Statue symbolizes the freedom enjoyed by all the people who settled in the United States. The United States was only thinly populated until the 17th century, when Europeans founded colonies in the east.

UNITED STATES

Christopher Columbus commanded the Santa Maria on his first voyage of discovery in 1492. He expected to reach India, but instead landed in the Bahamas. He mistakenly called the Native Americans Indians.

BAHAMAS

Gulf of Mexico

CUBA

DOMINICAN REPUBLIC

ANTIGUA AND BARBUDA

HAITI

ST KITTS AND NEVIS

ATLANTIC OCEAN

JAMAICA

DOMINICA
ST LUCIA

BARBADOS

ST VINCENT AND THE GRENADINES

GRENADA

TRINIDAD AND TOBAGO

MEXICO

BELIZE

Caribbean Sea

GUATEMALA

HONDURAS

EL SALVADOR

NICARAGUA

miles
0   500
0   500
kilometers

COSTA RICA   PANAMA

NORTH AMERICA
Area: 24,219,000 sq km (9,351,000 sq miles)
Population: 458,549,000
Number of independent countries: 23

5

CANADA AND GREENLAND

Canada is the world's second-largest country. Only Russia is bigger. Much of Canada has long, bitterly cold winters, and most Canadians live within 200 miles (320 km) of the southern border with the United States. The first people to live in Canada were Native Americans. But most Canadians today are descendants of French and British settlers.

Greenland is the world's largest island. It is a self-governing part of Denmark.

CANADA

Area: 9,976,139 sq km (3,851,809 sq miles)
Highest point: Mount Logan, 6,050 m (19,849 ft)
Population: 29,964,000
Capital: Ottawa (pop 312,000)
Largest cities: Toronto (4,264,000)
Montreal (3,327,000)
Vancouver (1,832,000)
Official languages: English, French
Religions: Roman Catholic 45%, Protestant 36%, Eastern Orthodox 2%, other 17%
Government: Federal constitutional monarchy
Currency: Canadian dollar

GREENLAND
Area: 2,175,600 sq km (840,000 sq miles)
Population: 58,000
Capital: Godthaab
Government: Self-governing part of Denmark.

ST PIERRE & MIQUELON
Area: 242 sq km (93 sq miles)
Population: 6,000
Capital: St. Pierre
Government: French territory

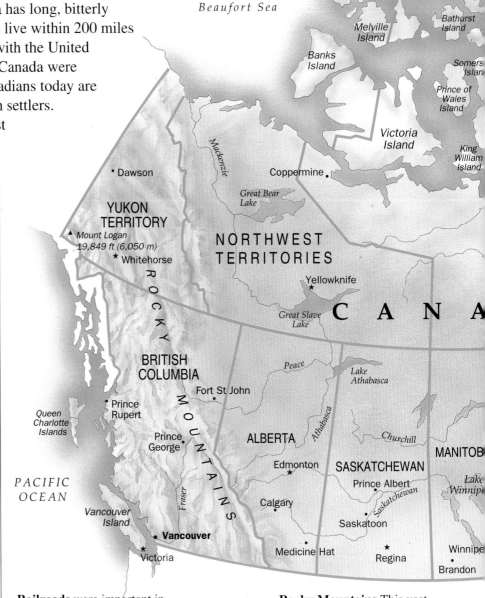

Beaufort Sea

Melville Island
Banks Island
Bathurst Island
Somers Island
Prince of Wales Island
Victoria Island
King William Island

• Dawson
Coppermine •

YUKON TERRITORY
Great Bear Lake
▲ Mount Logan 19,849 ft (6,050 m)
★ Whitehorse

NORTHWEST TERRITORIES

Yellowknife ★

C A N A

Great Slave Lake

BRITISH COLUMBIA
Peace
Lake Athabasca

• Prince Rupert
Fort St John •

Queen Charlotte Islands

• Prince George

ALBERTA
Churchill

SASKATCHEWAN
MANITOB

Edmonton ★
Prince Albert •
Lake Winnipe

PACIFIC OCEAN

Calgary •
Saskatoon

Vancouver Island
Medicine Hat •
Regina ★
Winnipe

• **Vancouver**
★ Victoria

• Brandon

Railroads were important in opening up the vast country of Canada. The two major companies are the government-owned Canadian National Railways (CN) and the privately owned Canadian Pacific (CP) Rail System.

Rocky Mountains This vast range in western Canada has much magnificent scenery. The Pacific Ranges rise to the west of the Rockies. Canada's highest peak, Mount Logan, is in the northwest.

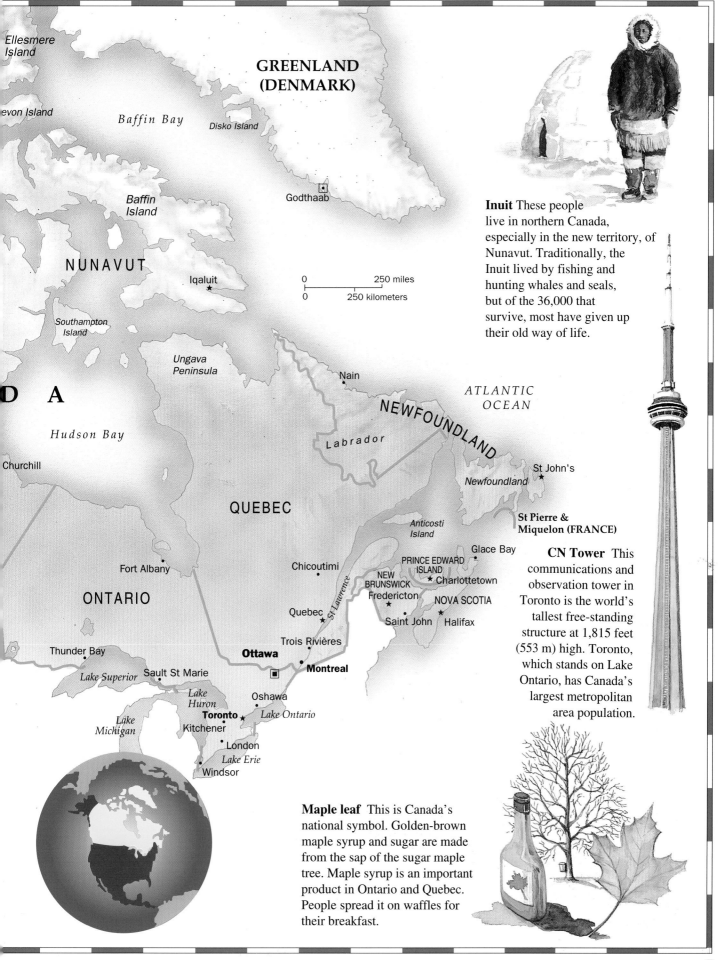

Ellesmere Island

evon Island

Baffin Bay

Disko Island

GREENLAND (DENMARK)

Baffin Island

Godthaab

NUNAVUT

Iqaluit ★

Southampton Island

Ungava Peninsula

0   250 miles

0   250 kilometers

D   A

Hudson Bay

Nain

ATLANTIC OCEAN

NEWFOUNDLAND

Labrador

Churchill

St John's ★

QUEBEC

Newfoundland

Anticosti Island

St Pierre & Miquelon (FRANCE)

Fort Albany

Chicoutimi

Glace Bay

PRINCE EDWARD ISLAND

ONTARIO

Quebec ★

St Lawrence

NEW BRUNSWICK

Fredericton ★

★ Charlottetown

NOVA SCOTIA

Saint John

Halifax

Trois Rivières

Thunder Bay

Ottawa

Montreal

Lake Superior

Sault St Marie

Lake Huron

Oshawa

Toronto ★

Lake Ontario

Lake Michigan

Kitchener

• London

Lake Erie

Windsor

Inuit These people live in northern Canada, especially in the new territory, of Nunavut. Traditionally, the Inuit lived by fishing and hunting whales and seals, but of the 36,000 that survive, most have given up their old way of life.

CN Tower This communications and observation tower in Toronto is the world's tallest free-standing structure at 1,815 feet (553 m) high. Toronto, which stands on Lake Ontario, has Canada's largest metropolitan area population.

Maple leaf This is Canada's national symbol. Golden-brown maple syrup and sugar are made from the sap of the sugar maple tree. Maple syrup is an important product in Ontario and Quebec. People spread it on waffles for their breakfast.

EASTERN CANADA

The four Atlantic provinces, together with Ontario and Quebec, make up eastern Canada. This region covers less than one-third of Canada, but it contains about 70 percent of the country's population. The most densely populated area extends along the shores of lakes Erie and Ontario and through the St Lawrence River valley. The river itself, together with several lakes, canals, and locks, form a major waterway called the St.Lawrence Seaway. This waterway is the outlet for the entire Great Lakes region.

Seals are found around the coasts of eastern Canada. Hunting of newborn harp seals for their fur has now been stopped.

Samuel de Champlain, a French explorer, helped to colonize French Canada in the early 17th century. Many Canadians still speak French, especially in the province of Quebec.

Beavers live in rivers and lakes in forested regions throughout eastern Canada. They gnaw down trees and use branches to build dams and lodges (homes) for their young in the water.

Hockey, also called ice hockey, is Canada's national sport. This fast and exciting game played on an ice rink began in Canada in the mid-19th century. It is now played in many countries.

Ungava Peninsula

Hudson Bay

James Bay

Fort Albany

ONTARIO

Kenora

Timmins

Thunder Bay

Lake Superior

Sault Ste. Marie

Lake Huron

Lake Michigan

Kitchener
Hamilton
London
Windsor

Toronto ★ Lake Ontario

Niagara Falls

Lake Erie

0		200 miles
0		200 kilometers

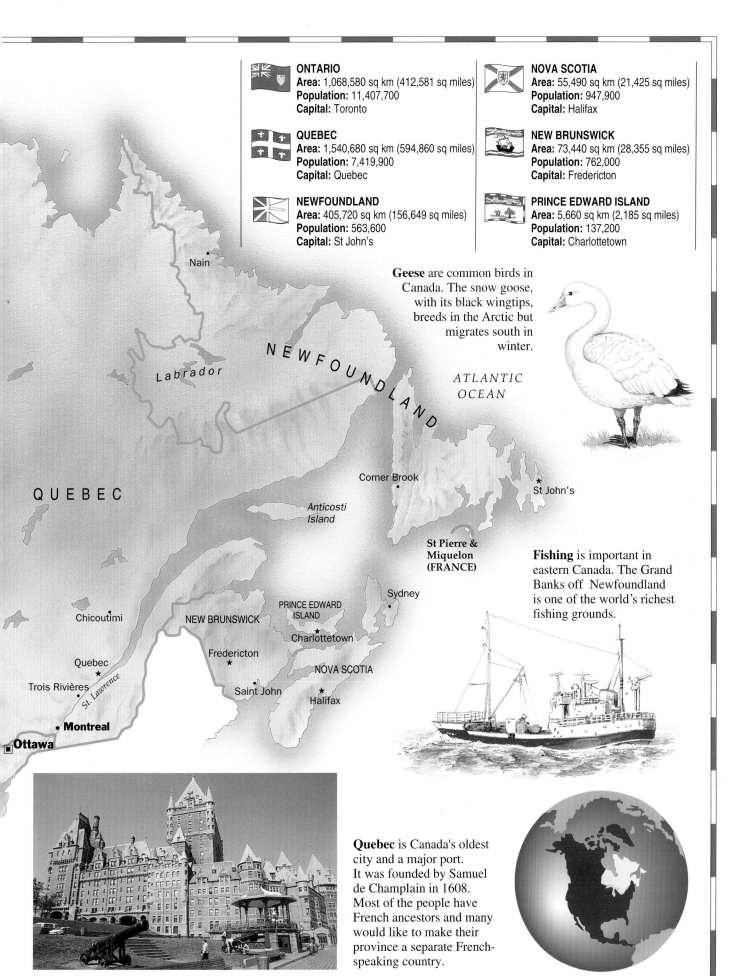

ONTARIO
Area: 1,068,580 sq km (412,581 sq miles)
Population: 11,407,700
Capital: Toronto

QUEBEC
Area: 1,540,680 sq km (594,860 sq miles)
Population: 7,419,900
Capital: Quebec

NEWFOUNDLAND
Area: 405,720 sq km (156,649 sq miles)
Population: 563,600
Capital: St John's

NOVA SCOTIA
Area: 55,490 sq km (21,425 sq miles)
Population: 947,900
Capital: Halifax

NEW BRUNSWICK
Area: 73,440 sq km (28,355 sq miles)
Population: 762,000
Capital: Fredericton

PRINCE EDWARD ISLAND
Area: 5,660 sq km (2,185 sq miles)
Population: 137,200
Capital: Charlottetown

Geese are common birds in Canada. The snow goose, with its black wingtips, breeds in the Arctic but migrates south in winter.

Nain

Labrador

N E W F O U N D L A N D

ATLANTIC
OCEAN

QUEBEC

Corner Brook

St John's

Anticosti
Island

St Pierre &
Miquelon
(FRANCE)

Sydney

Fishing is important in eastern Canada. The Grand Banks off Newfoundland is one of the world's richest fishing grounds.

Chicoutimi

NEW BRUNSWICK

PRINCE EDWARD
ISLAND

Charlottetown

Quebec

Fredericton

Trois Rivières

St. Lawrence

NOVA SCOTIA

Saint John

Halifax

Montreal

Ottawa

Quebec is Canada's oldest city and a major port. It was founded by Samuel de Champlain in 1608. Most of the people have French ancestors and many would like to make their province a separate French-speaking country.

9

WESTERN CANADA

Western Canada consists of four provinces — Alberta, British Columbia, Manitoba, and Saskatchewan — and three territories — Northwest Territories, Nunavut, which was created in 1999, and Yukon Territory. The provinces contain vast plains called prairies, towering mountains in the west, and the Pacific coast. The three territories in the north are thinly populated. Less than one percent of Canada's people lives there.

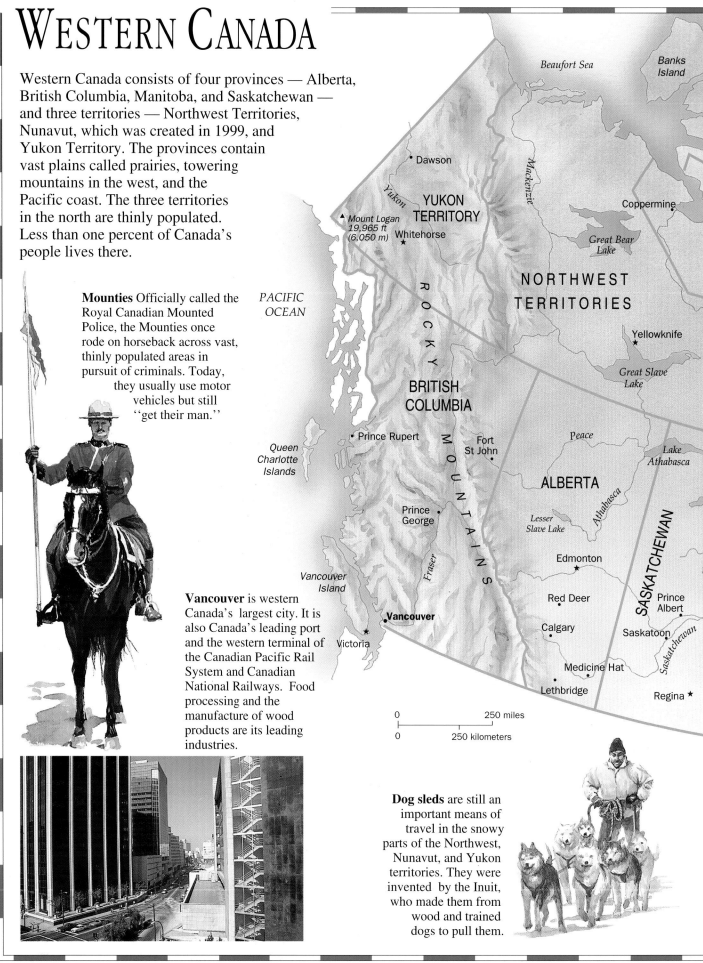

Mounties Officially called the Royal Canadian Mounted Police, the Mounties once rode on horseback across vast, thinly populated areas in pursuit of criminals. Today, they usually use motor vehicles but still ''get their man.''

Vancouver is western Canada's largest city. It is also Canada's leading port and the western terminal of the Canadian Pacific Rail System and Canadian National Railways. Food processing and the manufacture of wood products are its leading industries.

Beaufort Sea

Banks Island

Dawson

Yukon

YUKON TERRITORY

▲ Mount Logan 19,965 ft (6,050 m)

Whitehorse ★

Mackenzie

Coppermine

Great Bear Lake

NORTHWEST TERRITORIES

Yellowknife ★

PACIFIC OCEAN

R O C K Y

Great Slave Lake

BRITISH COLUMBIA

Prince Rupert

Fort St John

Peace

Lake Athabasca

Queen Charlotte Islands

M O U N T A I N S

ALBERTA

Athabasca

SASKATCHEWAN

Prince George

Lesser Slave Lake

Edmonton ★

Fraser

Vancouver Island

Red Deer

Prince Albert

Vancouver •

Calgary

Saskatoon

Saskatchewan

★ Victoria

Medicine Hat

Lethbridge

Regina ★

| 0 | | 250 miles |
| 0 | | 250 kilometers |

Dog sleds are still an important means of travel in the snowy parts of the Northwest, Nunavut, and Yukon territories. They were invented by the Inuit, who made them from wood and trained dogs to pull them.

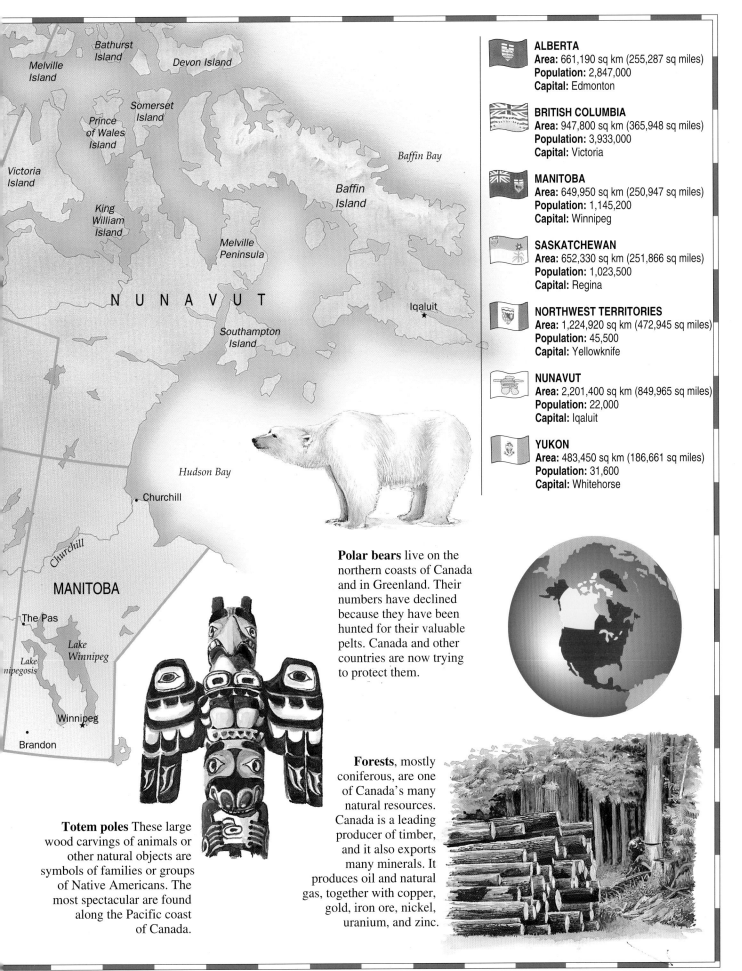

Melville Island
Bathurst Island
Devon Island

Somerset Island
Prince of Wales Island

Baffin Bay

Victoria Island

Baffin Island

King William Island

Melville Peninsula

N U N A V U T

Iqaluit
★

Southampton Island

Hudson Bay

•Churchill

Churchill

MANITOBA

•The Pas

Lake Winnipeg

Lake Winnipegosis

Winnipeg
★

•Brandon

ALBERTA
Area: 661,190 sq km (255,287 sq miles)
Population: 2,847,000
Capital: Edmonton

BRITISH COLUMBIA
Area: 947,800 sq km (365,948 sq miles)
Population: 3,933,000
Capital: Victoria

MANITOBA
Area: 649,950 sq km (250,947 sq miles)
Population: 1,145,200
Capital: Winnipeg

SASKATCHEWAN
Area: 652,330 sq km (251,866 sq miles)
Population: 1,023,500
Capital: Regina

NORTHWEST TERRITORIES
Area: 1,224,920 sq km (472,945 sq miles)
Population: 45,500
Capital: Yellowknife

NUNAVUT
Area: 2,201,400 sq km (849,965 sq miles)
Population: 22,000
Capital: Iqaluit

YUKON
Area: 483,450 sq km (186,661 sq miles)
Population: 31,600
Capital: Whitehorse

Polar bears live on the northern coasts of Canada and in Greenland. Their numbers have declined because they have been hunted for their valuable pelts. Canada and other countries are now trying to protect them.

Totem poles These large wood carvings of animals or other natural objects are symbols of families or groups of Native Americans. The most spectacular are found along the Pacific coast of Canada.

Forests, mostly coniferous, are one of Canada's many natural resources. Canada is a leading producer of timber, and it also exports many minerals. It produces oil and natural gas, together with copper, gold, iron ore, nickel, uranium, and zinc.

UNITED STATES OF AMERICA

The United States is the world's fourth-largest country but it ranks third in population. The country consists of 50 states, 48 of which form a large block between Canada and Mexico. The 49th state, Alaska, lies in the far northwest of North America, while the 50th, Hawaii, is a chain of volcanic islands in the north Pacific Ocean. The United States also includes the District of Columbia, the location of the capital city, Washington D.C.

George Washington, the first president of the United States (1789-97), led the Continental Army against the British in the American War of Independence, or RevolutionaryWar, (1775-83). Its victory led to the birth of the United States.

Native Americans were the first people to live in what is now the United States. They crossed from Asia into North America at least 10,000 years ago.

Landscapes The United States has large forests, grasslands, snow-capped mountains, and deserts. Much of the scenery is spectacular. Monument Valley on the Utah-Arizona border contains these remarkable rock formations.

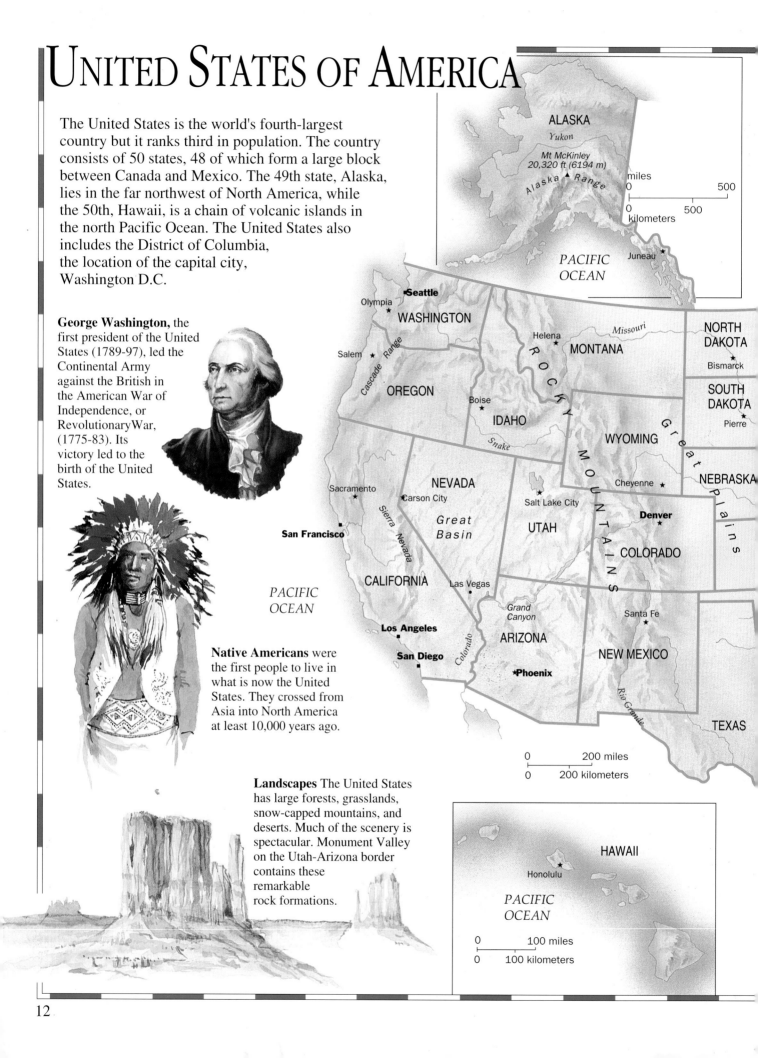

ALASKA
Yukon
Mt McKinley
20,320 ft (6194 m)
Alaska Range
miles
0   500
0   500
kilometers
PACIFIC OCEAN
Juneau

Seattle
Olympia
WASHINGTON
Salem
Cascade Range
OREGON
Boise
IDAHO
Snake
Helena
Missouri
MONTANA
ROCKY
WYOMING
Cheyenne
Great Plains
NORTH DAKOTA
Bismarck
SOUTH DAKOTA
Pierre
NEBRASKA

Sacramento
San Francisco
Sierra Nevada
NEVADA
Carson City
Great Basin
Salt Lake City
UTAH
MOUNTAINS
Denver
COLORADO

CALIFORNIA
Las Vegas
Grand Canyon
Colorado
ARIZONA
Phoenix
Santa Fe
NEW MEXICO
Rio Grande
TEXAS

Los Angeles
San Diego

PACIFIC OCEAN

0   200 miles
0   200 kilometers

HAWAII
Honolulu
PACIFIC OCEAN
0   100 miles
0   100 kilometers

12

UNITED STATES

Area: 9,529,063 sq km (3,679,192 sq miles)
Highest point: Mount McKinley, 6,194 m (20,320 ft)
Population: 265,284,000

Capital: Washington D.C. (pop 543,000)
Largest cities: New York City (7,381,000)
Los Angeles (3,554,000)
Chicago (2,722,000)
Official language: none (English is the chief language spoken in the United States, followed by Spanish)
Religions: Protestant 58%, Roman Catholic 21%, other Christians 6.4%, Jews 2.1%, Muslims 1.9%
Government: Federal republic
Currency: United States dollar

Bald eagle This majestic bird of prey was adopted as the national bird in 1782. Overhunting, pollution, and the destruction of wilderness areas threatened its survival. But it is now protected.

New York City The country's largest city has a magnificent skyline. It is popularly known as the "Big Apple" because it is a center of entertainment. It is also the nation's leading financial and business center.

Baseball is so popular that it has been called the national pastime of the United States. It was first played in the mid-18th century.

Exploring space U.S. Astronauts first landed on the moon in a lunar module in 1969. The United States is now using probes to explore Mars and the rest of the solar system.

13

NORTHEASTERN STATES

The northeastern states region includes the six New England states of Connecticut, Maine, Massachusetts, New Hampshire, Rhode Island, and Vermont. It also includes Delaware, Maryland, New Jersey, New York, and Pennsylvania. The map also shows the country's capital, Washington, which lies within an area called the District of Columbia. The Northeast contains fertile farmland, great industrial cities, and many historic sites.

New England is a historic region that formed part of the original 13 British colonies, which became the nucleus for the United States after the Revolutionary War of 1775–83. In the autumn New England's forests are ablaze with color.

Coal mines in Pennsylvania produced the fuel used by the state's great steel and machinery industries. Today, New York, Pennsylvania, and New Jersey rank among the country's top manufacturing states.

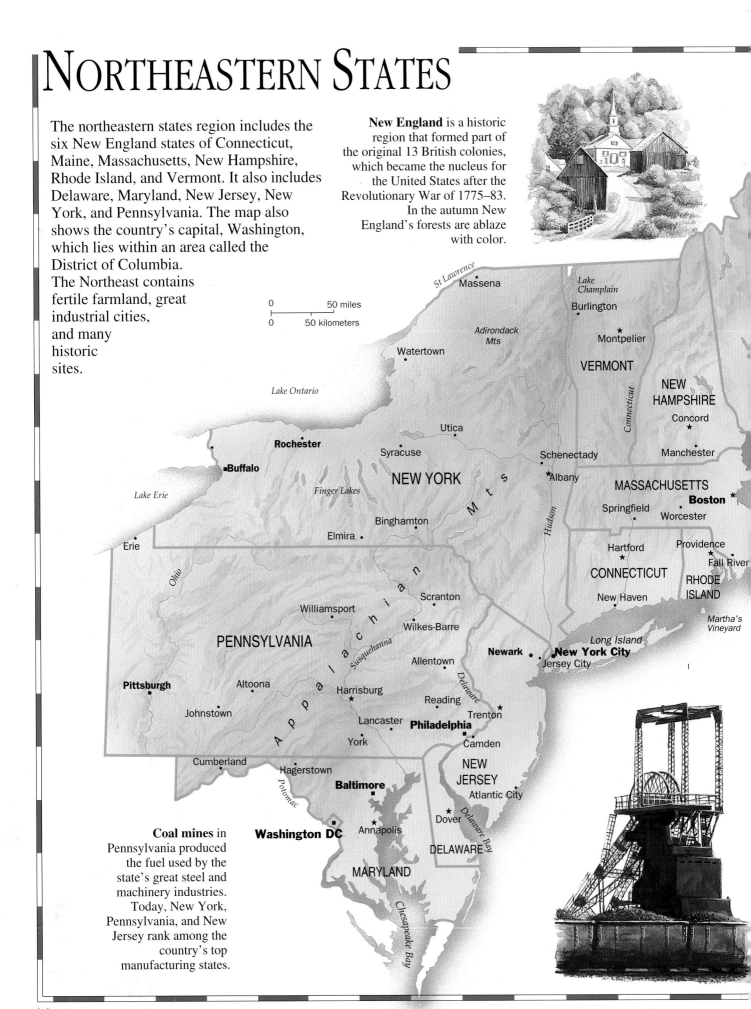

St Lawrence
Massena
Lake Champlain
Burlington
Adirondack Mts
Montpelier
Watertown
VERMONT
NEW HAMPSHIRE
Concord
Lake Ontario
Utica
Rochester
Syracuse
Schenectady
Manchester
Buffalo
NEW YORK
Albany
MASSACHUSETTS
Lake Erie
Finger Lakes
Springfield
Boston
Worcester
Binghamton
Hartford
Providence
Elmira
Fall River
Erie
Ohio
CONNECTICUT
RHODE ISLAND
New Haven
Martha's Vineyard
Scranton
Williamsport
Wilkes-Barre
Long Island
PENNSYLVANIA
Newark
New York City
Allentown
Jersey City
Pittsburgh
Altoona
Harrisburg
Reading
Johnstown
Lancaster
Trenton
Philadelphia
York
Camden
Cumberland
Hagerstown
NEW JERSEY
Baltimore
Atlantic City
Potomac
Dover
Washington DC
Annapolis
DELAWARE
MARYLAND
Delaware Bay
Chesapeake Bay

0   50 miles
0   50 kilometers

Presque Isle

Moosehead
Lake

MAINE

Bangor

Augusta
★

ATLANTIC
OCEAN

Portland

Cape Cod

Nantucket
Island

Capitol This is the building in Washington, D.C., where Congress (the Senate and the House of Representatives) meets. President George Washington laid its cornerstone in 1793, and Congress first met there in 1800.

Covered bridges have a roof and sides that protect the wooden structure from the weather. The first long covered bridge in the United States was built in Massachusetts in 1806.

Abraham Lincoln served as president of the United States between 1861 and 1865, when he was assassinated. He led the Union to victory in the Civil War (1861–65).

Liberty Bell This church bell in Philadelphia is a symbol of American freedom. It was rung on July 8, 1776, to announce the adoption of the Declaration of Independence. The bell broke in 1835 and is no longer rung.

 CONNECTICUT
Area: 12,997 sq km (5,018 sq miles)
Population: 3,274,000
Capital: Hartford

 DELAWARE
Area: 5,294 sq km (2,045 sq miles)
Population: 725,000
Capital: Dover

 MAINE
Area: 86,156 sq km (33,265 sq miles)
Population: 1,243,000
Capital: Augusta

 MARYLAND
Area: 27,091 sq km (10,460 sq miles)
Population: 5,072,000
Capital: Annapolis

 MASSACHUSETTS
Area: 21,455 sq km (8,284 sq miles)
Population: 6,092,000
Capital: Boston

 NEW HAMPSHIRE
Area: 24,032 sq km (9,279 sq miles)
Population: 1,162,000
Capital: Concord

 NEW JERSEY
Area: 20,168 sq km (7,787 sq miles)
Population: 7,988,000
Capital: Trenton

 NEW YORK
Area: 136,583 sq km (52,735 sq miles)
Population: 18,185,000
Capital: Albany

 PENNSYLVANIA
Area: 119,251 sq km (46,043 sq miles)
Population: 12,056,000
Capital: Harrisburg

 RHODE ISLAND
Area: 3,139 sq km (1,212 sq miles)
Population: 990,000
Capital: Providence

 VERMONT
Area: 24,900 sq km (9,614 sq miles)
Population: 589,000
Capital: Montpelier

 DISTRICT OF COLUMBIA
Area: 179 sq km (69 sq miles)
Population: 543,000

SOUTHEASTERN STATES

The southeastern states contain large areas of coastal plains and the southern part of the scenic Appalachian Mountains. The region is rich in history. Virginia, North and South Carolina, and Georgia were among the 13 English colonies that formed the nucleus of the United States, while the region was the major theater in the Civil War. The states once depended on farming, but manufacturing is now important.

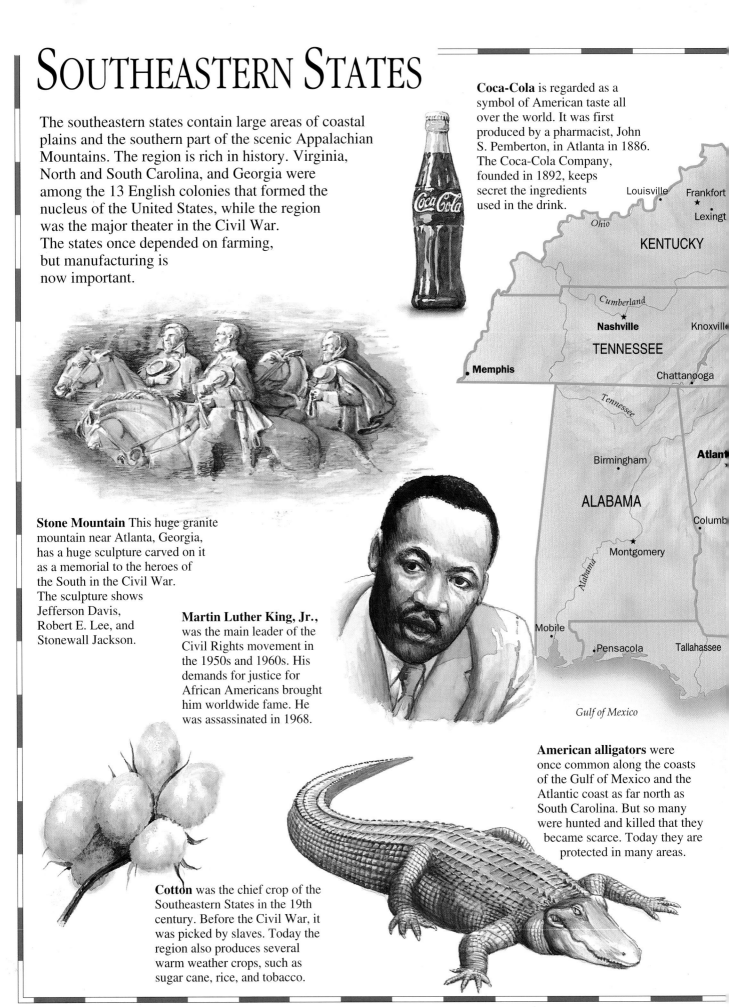

Coca-Cola is regarded as a symbol of American taste all over the world. It was first produced by a pharmacist, John S. Pemberton, in Atlanta in 1886. The Coca-Cola Company, founded in 1892, keeps secret the ingredients used in the drink.

Louisville
Frankfort
Lexingt
Ohio
KENTUCKY

Cumberland
Nashville
Knoxvill
TENNESSEE
Memphis
Chattanooga
Tennessee

Birmingham
Atlant
ALABAMA
Columb
Montgomery
Alabama
Mobile
Pensacola
Tallahassee

Gulf of Mexico

Stone Mountain This huge granite mountain near Atlanta, Georgia, has a huge sculpture carved on it as a memorial to the heroes of the South in the Civil War. The sculpture shows Jefferson Davis, Robert E. Lee, and Stonewall Jackson.

Martin Luther King, Jr., was the main leader of the Civil Rights movement in the 1950s and 1960s. His demands for justice for African Americans brought him worldwide fame. He was assassinated in 1968.

American alligators were once common along the coasts of the Gulf of Mexico and the Atlantic coast as far north as South Carolina. But so many were hunted and killed that they became scarce. Today they are protected in many areas.

Cotton was the chief crop of the Southeastern States in the 19th century. Before the Civil War, it was picked by slaves. Today the region also produces several warm weather crops, such as sugar cane, rice, and tobacco.

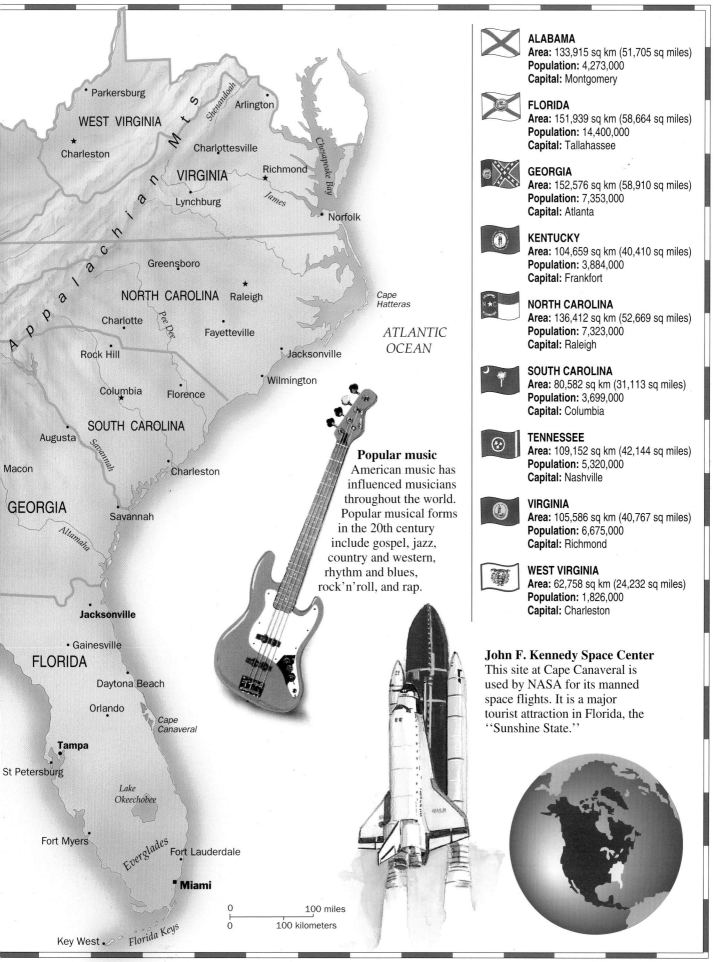

ALABAMA
Area: 133,915 sq km (51,705 sq miles)
Population: 4,273,000
Capital: Montgomery

FLORIDA
Area: 151,939 sq km (58,664 sq miles)
Population: 14,400,000
Capital: Tallahassee

GEORGIA
Area: 152,576 sq km (58,910 sq miles)
Population: 7,353,000
Capital: Atlanta

KENTUCKY
Area: 104,659 sq km (40,410 sq miles)
Population: 3,884,000
Capital: Frankfort

NORTH CAROLINA
Area: 136,412 sq km (52,669 sq miles)
Population: 7,323,000
Capital: Raleigh

SOUTH CAROLINA
Area: 80,582 sq km (31,113 sq miles)
Population: 3,699,000
Capital: Columbia

TENNESSEE
Area: 109,152 sq km (42,144 sq miles)
Population: 5,320,000
Capital: Nashville

VIRGINIA
Area: 105,586 sq km (40,767 sq miles)
Population: 6,675,000
Capital: Richmond

WEST VIRGINIA
Area: 62,758 sq km (24,232 sq miles)
Population: 1,826,000
Capital: Charleston

Popular music
American music has influenced musicians throughout the world. Popular musical forms in the 20th century include gospel, jazz, country and western, rhythm and blues, rock'n'roll, and rap.

John F. Kennedy Space Center
This site at Cape Canaveral is used by NASA for its manned space flights. It is a major tourist attraction in Florida, the "Sunshine State."

ATLANTIC OCEAN

0   100 miles
0   100 kilometers

SOUTH-CENTRAL STATES

Arkansas, Louisiana, and Mississippi, which form the eastern part of the south-central states, are drained by the Mississippi River valley. In the west lie the vast open spaces of Texas and Oklahoma. These two states, together with Louisiana, are among the top five petroleum producers in the United States. The region also contains some major cities, including Houston, San Antonio and Dallas, which are among the country's ten largest.

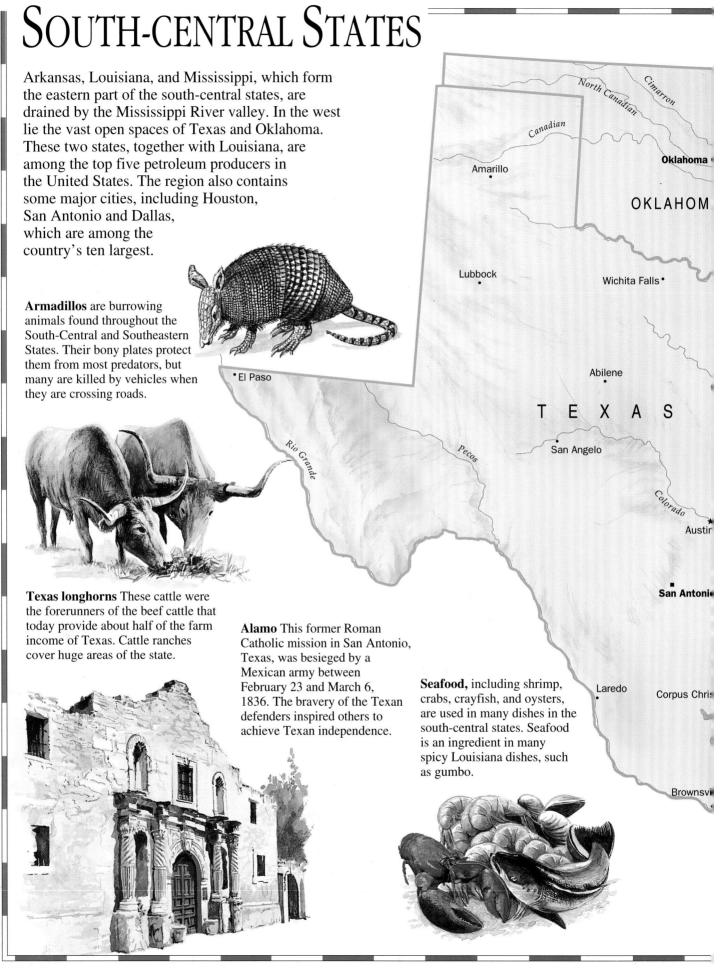

Armadillos are burrowing animals found throughout the South-Central and Southeastern States. Their bony plates protect them from most predators, but many are killed by vehicles when they are crossing roads.

Texas longhorns These cattle were the forerunners of the beef cattle that today provide about half of the farm income of Texas. Cattle ranches cover huge areas of the state.

Alamo This former Roman Catholic mission in San Antonio, Texas, was besieged by a Mexican army between February 23 and March 6, 1836. The bravery of the Texan defenders inspired others to achieve Texan independence.

Seafood, including shrimp, crabs, crayfish, and oysters, are used in many dishes in the south-central states. Seafood is an ingredient in many spicy Louisiana dishes, such as gumbo.

Amarillo

Oklahoma

OKLAHOM

Lubbock

Wichita Falls

Abilene

El Paso

T E X A S

San Angelo

Rio Grande

Pecos

Colorado

Austir

San Antoni

Laredo

Corpus Chris

Brownsv

North Canadian

Cimarron

Canadian

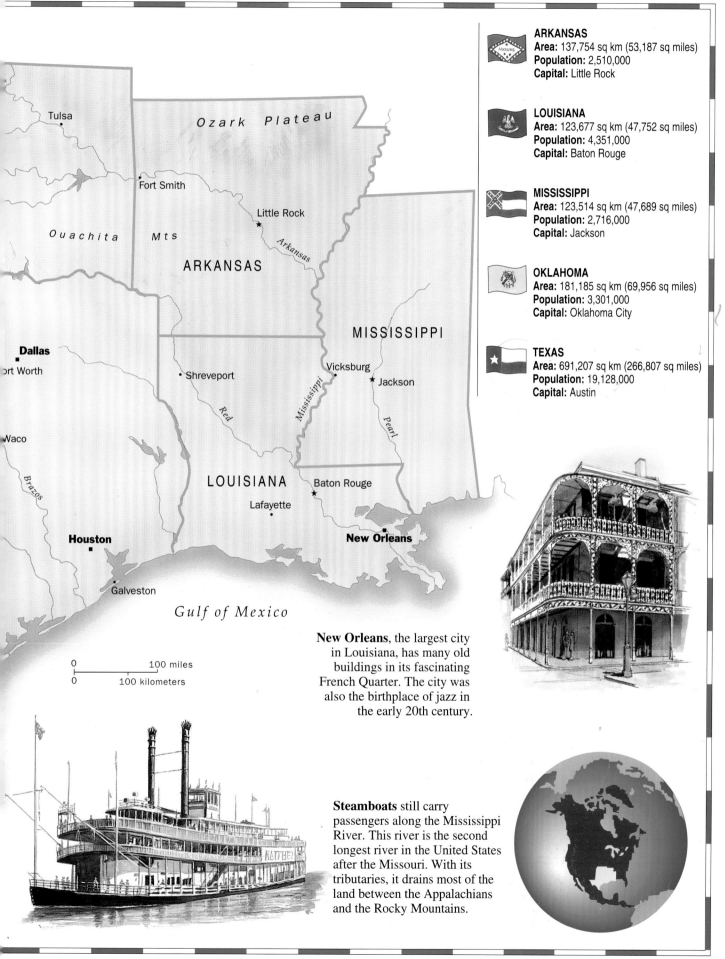

Tulsa

Ozark Plateau

Fort Smith

Little Rock ★

Arkansas

Ouachita Mts

ARKANSAS

Dallas

rt Worth

Shreveport

Vicksburg

MISSISSIPPI

Jackson ★

Red

Mississippi

Pearl

Waco

Brazos

LOUISIANA

Baton Rouge ★

Lafayette

Houston

New Orleans

Galveston

Gulf of Mexico

| 0 | 100 miles |
| 0 | 100 kilometers |

ARKANSAS
Area: 137,754 sq km (53,187 sq miles)
Population: 2,510,000
Capital: Little Rock

LOUISIANA
Area: 123,677 sq km (47,752 sq miles)
Population: 4,351,000
Capital: Baton Rouge

MISSISSIPPI
Area: 123,514 sq km (47,689 sq miles)
Population: 2,716,000
Capital: Jackson

OKLAHOMA
Area: 181,185 sq km (69,956 sq miles)
Population: 3,301,000
Capital: Oklahoma City

TEXAS
Area: 691,207 sq km (266,807 sq miles)
Population: 19,128,000
Capital: Austin

New Orleans, the largest city in Louisiana, has many old buildings in its fascinating French Quarter. The city was also the birthplace of jazz in the early 20th century.

Steamboats still carry passengers along the Mississippi River. This river is the second longest river in the United States after the Missouri. With its tributaries, it drains most of the land between the Appalachians and the Rocky Mountains.

19

MIDWESTERN STATES

The 12 midwestern states cover about one-fifth of the United States. The land is mostly flat, including parts of the Great Plains in the west and the lower interior plains south and west of the Great Lakes. Farmers produce grains and other crops on the fertile land, together with dairy products and livestock. Major industrial cities include Chicago, Detroit, and Indianapolis. The Great Lakes and the Mississippi River are used to transport goods.

Bison once roamed the Great Plains in huge herds, but hunters slaughtered most of them. Today a few thousand live in protected areas.

Mount Rushmore National Memorial, South Dakota, is a carving of four presidents: George Washington, Thomas Jefferson, Theodore Roosevelt, and Abraham Lincoln. Each face is about 60 feet (18 m) high.

American football is played by high school and college teams. The professional National Football League is divided into the American Football Conference and the National Football Conference.

Pioneers had reached the Mississippi by the 1820s. In the 1840s wagon trains crossed the Great Plains. By the 1890s, scattered settlements had sprung up all across this dry region.

NORTH DAKOTA

Red Lake

Lake Sakakawea

Fargo

Duluth

★ Bismarck

MINNESOTA

Great Plains

SOUTH DAKOTA

Minneapolis ★ St Paul

Mississippi

Lake Oahe

Pierre ★

Black Hills

▲ Mt. Rushmore

Sioux Falls

Missouri

Sioux City

Cedar Rapid

IOWA

★ Des Moines

NEBRASKA

Platte

Omaha

Lincoln ★

Kansas

Kansas City

Topeka ★

KANSAS

Jefferson City ★

MISSOUR

Wichita

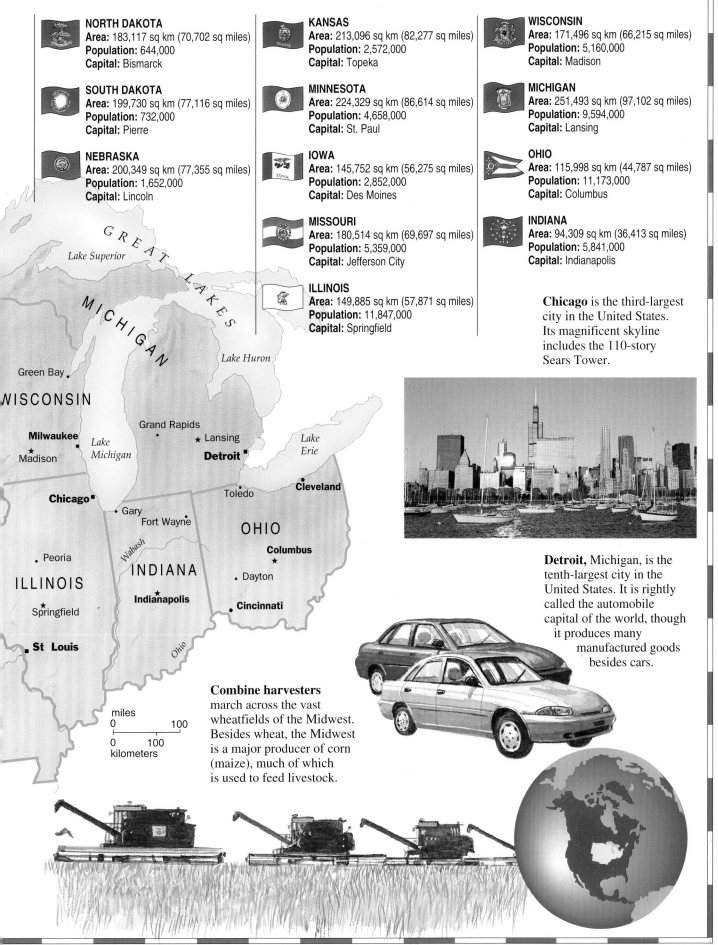

NORTH DAKOTA
Area: 183,117 sq km (70,702 sq miles)
Population: 644,000
Capital: Bismarck

SOUTH DAKOTA
Area: 199,730 sq km (77,116 sq miles)
Population: 732,000
Capital: Pierre

NEBRASKA
Area: 200,349 sq km (77,355 sq miles)
Population: 1,652,000
Capital: Lincoln

KANSAS
Area: 213,096 sq km (82,277 sq miles)
Population: 2,572,000
Capital: Topeka

MINNESOTA
Area: 224,329 sq km (86,614 sq miles)
Population: 4,658,000
Capital: St. Paul

IOWA
Area: 145,752 sq km (56,275 sq miles)
Population: 2,852,000
Capital: Des Moines

MISSOURI
Area: 180,514 sq km (69,697 sq miles)
Population: 5,359,000
Capital: Jefferson City

ILLINOIS
Area: 149,885 sq km (57,871 sq miles)
Population: 11,847,000
Capital: Springfield

WISCONSIN
Area: 171,496 sq km (66,215 sq miles)
Population: 5,160,000
Capital: Madison

MICHIGAN
Area: 251,493 sq km (97,102 sq miles)
Population: 9,594,000
Capital: Lansing

OHIO
Area: 115,998 sq km (44,787 sq miles)
Population: 11,173,000
Capital: Columbus

INDIANA
Area: 94,309 sq km (36,413 sq miles)
Population: 5,841,000
Capital: Indianapolis

Chicago is the third-largest city in the United States. Its magnificent skyline includes the 110-story Sears Tower.

Detroit, Michigan, is the tenth-largest city in the United States. It is rightly called the automobile capital of the world, though it produces many manufactured goods besides cars.

Combine harvesters march across the vast wheatfields of the Midwest. Besides wheat, the Midwest is a major producer of corn (maize), much of which is used to feed livestock.

miles
0   100
0   100
kilometers

NORTHWESTERN STATES

The eastern part of the northwestern states is part of the flat Great Plains. But the west is largely mountainous. The Cascade Range in Oregon and Washington has active volcanoes, including Mount Saint Helens, which exploded with great force in 1980, killing 57 people. Alaska, which became the 49th state on January 3, 1959, also has active volcanoes. Alaska is rich in oil, while farming and forestry are important in the other five states.

Aircraft Commercial and military aircraft as well as other military hardware are made by the Boeing Company, which has its headquarters in Seattle, Washington. The manufacture of wood products and processed foods are other major industries in the northwest.

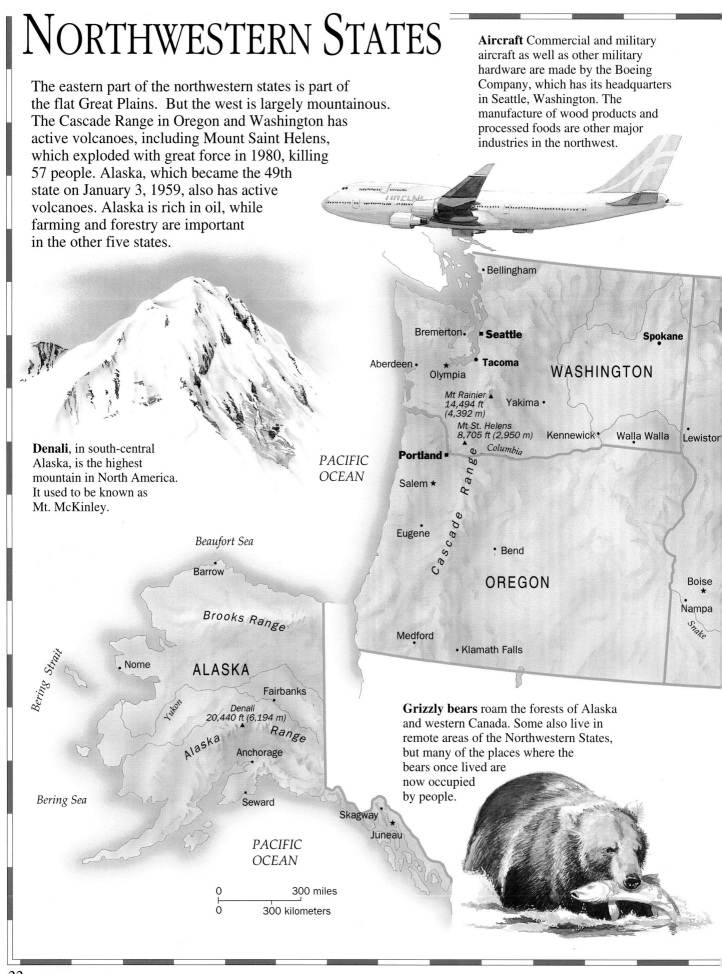

Denali, in south-central Alaska, is the highest mountain in North America. It used to be known as Mt. McKinley.

Grizzly bears roam the forests of Alaska and western Canada. Some also live in remote areas of the Northwestern States, but many of the places where the bears once lived are now occupied by people.

Bellingham

Bremerton • ■ **Seattle** **Spokane**

Aberdeen • ★ • **Tacoma** WASHINGTON
Olympia

Mt Rainier ▲ Yakima •
14,494 ft
(4,392 m)

Mt St. Helens
8,705 ft (2,950 m) Kennewick • Walla Walla Lewistor

Portland ■ Columbia

Salem ★

Eugene

• Bend

OREGON Boise ★

Nampa

Snake

Medford

• Klamath Falls

Cascade Range

PACIFIC OCEAN

Beaufort Sea

Barrow

Brooks Range

Bering Strait

• Nome ALASKA

Fairbanks

Denali
20,440 ft (6,194 m) Range

Yukon

Alaska

Anchorage

Bering Sea

Seward

Skagway
★
Juneau

PACIFIC OCEAN

```
0          300 miles
|——|——|——|
0          300 kilometers
```

ALASKA
Area: 1,530,693 sq km
(591,004 sq miles)
Population: 607,000
Capital: Juneau

IDAHO
Area: 216,430 sq km (83,564 sq miles)
Population: 1,189,000
Capital: Boise

MONTANA
Area: 380,849 sq km
(147,046 sq miles)
Population: 879,000
Capital: Helena

OREGON
Area: 251,418 sq km (97,073 sq miles)
Population: 3,204,000
Capital: Salem

WASHINGTON
Area: 176,479 sq km (68,139 sq miles)
Population: 5,553,000
Capital: Olympia

WYOMING
Area: 253,324 sq km (97,809 sq miles)
Population: 481,000
Capital: Cheyenne

Native Americans in the Northwest fished and hunted animals. They also gathered plant foods in the forests. They used wood to build houses and boats and to make containers, bowls, utensils, and masks like this one.

Yellowstone National Park lies mainly in northwestern Wyoming. It was set up in 1872 and is the world's oldest national park. It contains hot springs and geysers, canyons, and huge waterfalls.

0   100 miles
0   100 kilometers

Devils Tower, in northeastern Wyoming, is a mountain formed from hard volcanic rock. It rises 264 m (865 ft) from its base. It became the country's first national monument in 1906.

SOUTHWESTERN STATES

The southwestern states contain much magnificent scenery. California has more people than any other state and is the country's leading manufacturing and farming state. It also has valuable mineral deposits, including oil and natural gas. If California were a separate country, it would rank among the world's top ten in terms of the total value of the goods and services it produces. Hawaii, in the Pacific Ocean, became the 50th state on August 21, 1959.

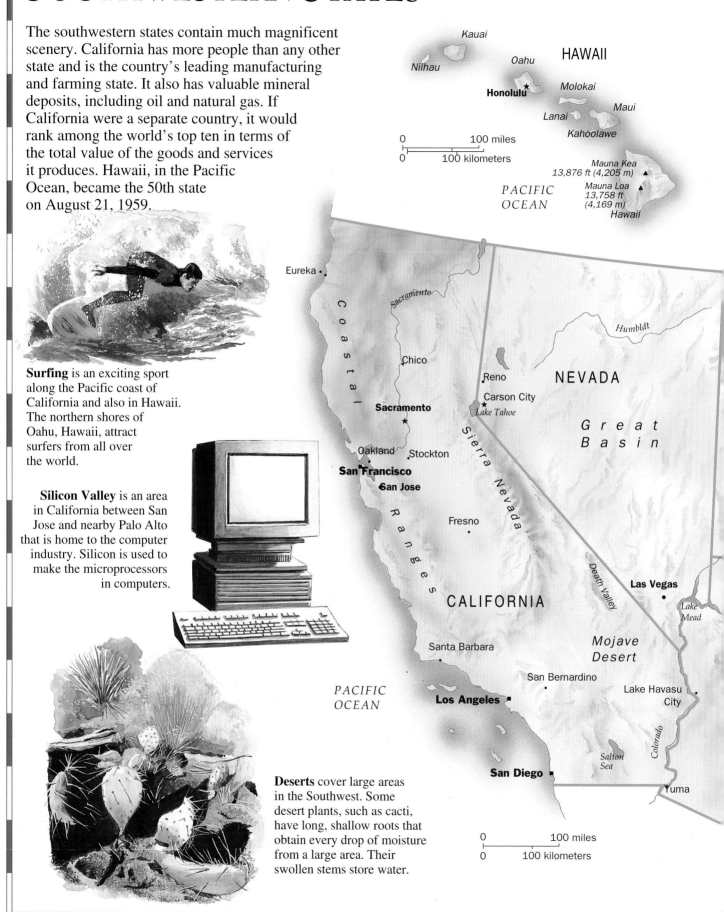

Surfing is an exciting sport along the Pacific coast of California and also in Hawaii. The northern shores of Oahu, Hawaii, attract surfers from all over the world.

Silicon Valley is an area in California between San Jose and nearby Palo Alto that is home to the computer industry. Silicon is used to make the microprocessors in computers.

Deserts cover large areas in the Southwest. Some desert plants, such as cacti, have long, shallow roots that obtain every drop of moisture from a large area. Their swollen stems store water.

HAWAII

Kauai

Niihau

Oahu

Honolulu ★

Molokai

Lanai

Maui

Kahoolawe

Mauna Kea
13,876 ft (4,205 m) ▲

Mauna Loa
13,758 ft
(4,169 m) ▲

Hawaii

PACIFIC
OCEAN

0 — 100 miles
0 — 100 kilometers

Eureka •

Sacramento

Chico

Reno •

Carson City ★
Lake Tahoe

NEVADA

Humbldt

Great
Basin

Sacramento ★

Oakland Stockton •

San Francisco

San Jose

Sierra Nevada

Coastal Ranges

Fresno •

Death Valley

Las Vegas •

Lake
Mead

CALIFORNIA

Mojave
Desert

Santa Barbara •

San Bernardino •

Lake Havasu
City •

Los Angeles ■

Colorado

PACIFIC
OCEAN

Salton
Sea

San Diego ■

Yuma

0 — 100 miles
0 — 100 kilometers

Kilauea is an active volcano on the eastern slope of Mauna Loa, Hawaii. It emits runny lava that flows down to the sea. All of the islands in Hawaii were formed by volcanoes. But only the volcanoes on Hawaii itself are active. The others are extinct.

Grand Canyon This huge canyon was worn out by the Colorado River and is around 1.6 km (1mile) deep in places. The canyon, like many of the country's scenic wonders, is protected in a national park.

ARIZONA
Area: 295,259 sq km (114,000 sq miles)
Population: 4,428,000
Capital: Phoenix

CALIFORNIA
Area: 411,047 sq km (158,706 sq miles)
Population: 31,878,000
Capital: Sacramento

COLORADO
Area: 269,594 sq km (104,091 sq miles)
Population: 3,823,000
Capital: Denver

HAWAII
Area: 16,760 sq km (6,471 sq miles)
Population: 1,184,000
Capital: Honolulu

NEVADA
Area: 286,352 sq km (110,561 sq miles)
Population: 1,603,000
Capital: Carson City

NEW MEXICO
Area: 314,924 sq km (121,593 sq miles)
Population: 1,713,000
Capital: Santa Fe

UTAH
Area: 219,887 sq km (84,899 sq miles)
Population: 2,000,000
Capital: Salt Lake City

Mesa Verde is a national park in southwestern Colorado. Its name means ''green table,'' and it contains impressive remains of cliff dwellings built by Native Americans hundreds of years ago.

MEXICO

Mexico, the third-largest country in North America, forms a bridge between the United States and the seven countries of Central America. The land is mainly mountainous, with deserts in the north and rainforests in the south. Temperatures vary according to the height of the land. Farming is important, but Mexico's main exports are oil and oil products. Factories in the north assemble goods, such as vehicle parts, for US companies.

MEXICO

Area: 1,972,547 sq km (761,605 sq miles)
Highest point: Citlalt petl (also called Orizaba), 5,700 m (18,701 ft)
Population: 93,182,000
Capital: Mexico City (pop 15,643,000)
Other large cities: Guadalajara (2,847,000)
Monterrey (2,522,000)
Puebla (1,055,000)
Official language: Spanish
Religions: Roman Catholic 90%, Protestant 5%, other 5%
Government: Federal republic
Currency: Mexican peso

Tarantula is the popular name given to large, hairy spiders of the family Theraphosidae, which are found between the southwestern United States and South America. They look frightening, but their bite is generally not serious.

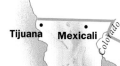

Tijuana · Mexicali · *Colorado* · Ciudad Juárez

Hermosillo · *Sierra Madre Occidental* · Chihuahua

Baja California · *Gulf of California* · Culiacán · Durango

La Paz · Mazatlán

PACIFIC OCEAN

Tepic

Monarch butterfly This colorful creature holds the record among insects for the distance it migrates each year. In autumn, it travels from New England to the southern United States and Mexico. In spring it returns to the north.

Acapulco is Mexico's leading Pacific Ocean resort. Tourism is a major industry in Mexico. Some people come to the seaside resorts while others want to see the great Native American historic sites.

Gold and silver objects made by Aztecs are evidence of their artistic skills. According to legend, the Aztec capital, Tenochtitlán, was founded in 1325. The Aztecs were defeated by the Spanish in 1521.

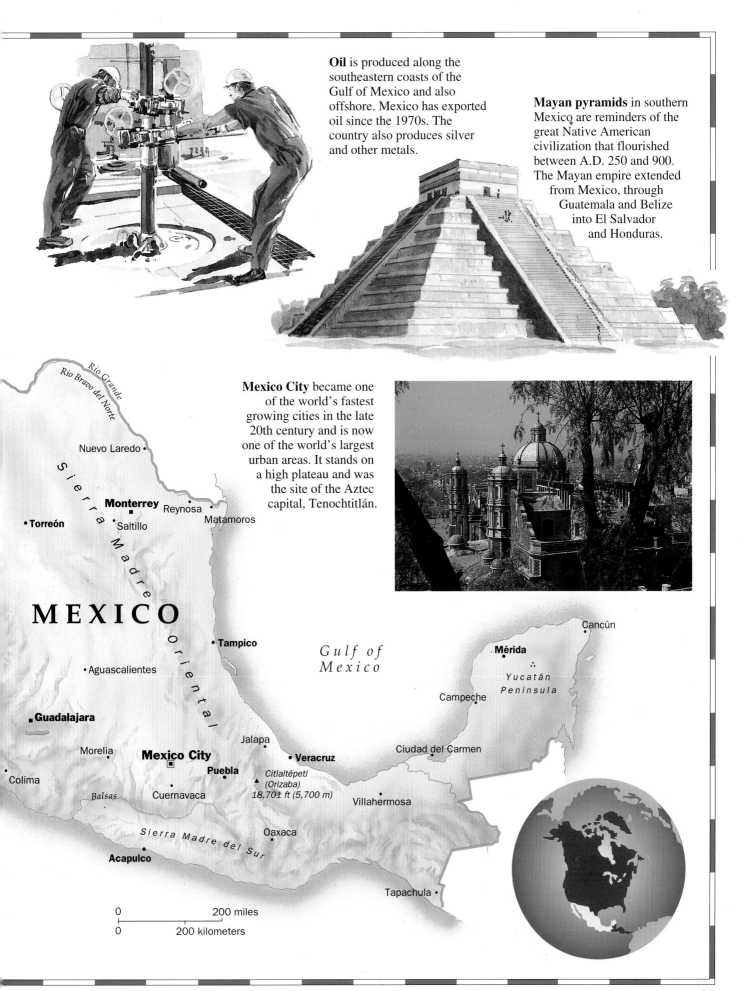

Oil is produced along the southeastern coasts of the Gulf of Mexico and also offshore. Mexico has exported oil since the 1970s. The country also produces silver and other metals.

Mayan pyramids in southern Mexico are reminders of the great Native American civilization that flourished between A.D. 250 and 900. The Mayan empire extended from Mexico, through Guatemala and Belize into El Salvador and Honduras.

Mexico City became one of the world's fastest growing cities in the late 20th century and is now one of the world's largest urban areas. It stands on a high plateau and was the site of the Aztec capital, Tenochtitlán.

Río Grande

Río Bravo del Norte

Nuevo Laredo

Sierra Madre Oriental

Monterrey · Reynosa

· **Torreón** · Saltillo · Matamoros

MEXICO

· **Tampico**

Gulf of Mexico

· Aguascalientes

· **Mérida**

Yucatán Peninsula

Guadalajara

Campeche

Morelia · **Mexico City** · Jalapa

Ciudad del Carmen

· **Veracruz**

· Colima **Puebla** Citlaltépetl (Orizaba) 18,701 ft (5,700 m)

Balsas Cuernavaca Villahermosa

Sierra Madre del Sur Oaxaca

Acapulco

Tapachula ·

0	200 miles
0	200 kilometers

27

WESTERN CENTRAL AMERICA

Western Central America consists of four countries: Belize, El Salvador, Guatemala, and Honduras. Hot and humid coasts border the region in the north and south. Between lies a highland zone with many active volcanoes. The people include Native Americans, together with people of African and European descent. Many people are of mixed origin. Farming is the main activity. Most people live in the cooler highlands.

Coral reefs and islands stretch along the swampy coast of Belize. They form the world's second-longest barrier reef after Australia's Graet Barrier Reef, and they are an important breeding area for fish.

 BELIZE

Area: 22,965 sq km (8,867 sq miles)
Population: 222,000
Capital: Belmopan (pop. 5,000)
Largest city: Belize City (48,000)
Government: Constitutional monarchy
Official language: English
Currency: Belize dollar

 EL SALVADOR

Area: 21,041 sq km (8,124 sq miles)
Population: 5,810,000
Capital and largest city: San Salvador (pop. 1,522,000)
Government: Republic
Official language: Spanish
Currency: Colón

 GUATEMALA

Area: 108,889 sq km (42,042 sq miles)
Population: 10,928,000
Capital and largest city: Guatemala City (pop. 2,000,000)
Government: Republic
Official language: Spanish
Currency: Quetzal

 HONDURAS

Area: 112,088 sq km (43,277 sq miles)
Population: 6,101,000
Capital and largest city: Tegucigalpa (pop. 679,000)
Government: Republic
Official language: Spanish
Currency: Lempira

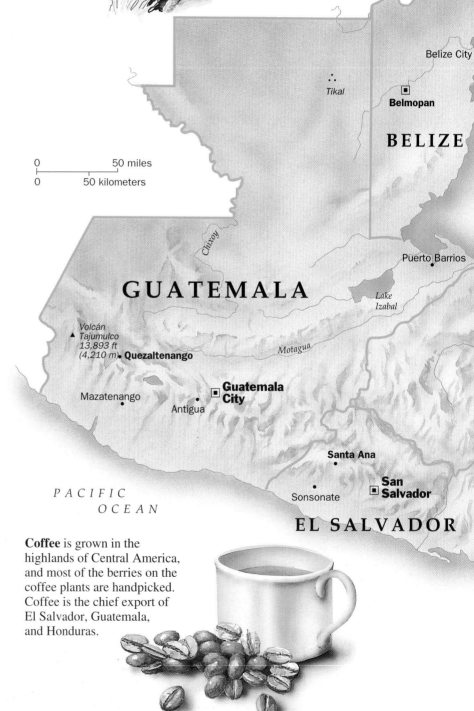

0   50 miles
0   50 kilometers

Belize City
Tikal
Belmopan
BELIZE
Chixoy
Puerto Barrios
GUATEMALA
Lake Izabal
Volcán Tajumulco 13,893 ft (4,210 m)
Quezaltenango
Motagua
Mazatenango
Guatemala City
Antigua
Santa Ana
San Salvador
Sonsonate
PACIFIC OCEAN
EL SALVADOR

Coffee is grown in the highlands of Central America, and most of the berries on the coffee plants are handpicked. Coffee is the chief export of El Salvador, Guatemala, and Honduras.

Tikal, in northern Guatemala, contains huge ruined pyramids. It was the biggest city of the Maya. Its main temple stood on top of a pyramid 150 feet (45 m) tall.

Bananas grow well in hot, wet climates, and they are a leading crop on the lowlands of Central America. The other main crop grown for export in lowland areas is sugarcane.

Caribbean Sea

Gulf of Honduras

Islas de la Bahia

Tela

La Ceiba

San Pedro Sula

Patuca

Juticalpa

HONDURAS

Tegucigalpa

n Miguel

Manatees, or sea cows, live along the Caribbean coasts of Central America and northern South America. Found in sheltered coastal waters, they have suffered from the effects of pollution and the use of power boats.

Market days in Guatemalan towns and villages are lively occasions when farmers bring their products for sale. About 45 percent of Guatemala's people are direct descendants of the original Native Americans.

29

EASTERN CENTRAL AMERICA

Like Western Central America, Costa Rica, Nicaragua, and Panama have hot, tropical climates except in highland areas, which are cooler. Nicaragua is the largest country in Central America. Like Costa Rica, it lies in an unstable area where earthquakes and volcanic eruptions are common. Costa Rica has many beautiful national parks and now attracts many tourists. Panama is an isthmus, a narrow strip of land that links North and South America,

COSTA RICA

Area: 50,700 sq km (19,575 sq miles)
Population: 3,442,000
Capital: San Jos
Largest city: San Jos (1,186,000)
Government: Republic
Official language: Spanish
Religions: Christianity (Roman Catholic 80%)
Currency: Costa Rican colón

NICARAGUA

Area: 130,000 sq km (50,193 sq miles)
Population: 6,101,000
Capital: Managua
Largest city: Managua (974,000)
Government: Republic
Official language: Spanish
Religions: Christianity (Roman Catholic 77%)
Currency: Córdoba

PANAMA

Area: 77,082 sq km (29,762 sq miles)
Population: 2,674,000
Capital: Panama City
Largest city: Panama City (452,000)
Government: Republic
Official language: Spanish
Religions: Christianity (Roman Catholic 80%)
Currency: Balboa

Pan-American Highway
This road system extends through the Americas from the United States border to southern Chile. The only break is in Panama, where the road is blocked by dense rainforest.

Active volcanoes Vocanic eruptions are common throughout the highlands of Nicaragua and Costa Rica. The volcanic rocks have weathered to produce rich, fertile soils.

Rainforests once covered most of the region. But large areas of forest have been cut down to create farmland, towns, factories, and so on. The destruction of forests has caused a great loss of tropical plants and animals.

Emerald toucanets live in forests from southern Mexico to Peru. They are noisy birds, but their green plumage makes them hard to see. Central America is rich in birdlife, with species from both North and South America.

Panama Canal This waterway links the Atlantic and Pacific oceans, keeping ships from having to sail around South America. The Canal was completed in 1914. It is almost 82 km (51 miles) long.

Caribbean Sea

Puerto Limón

• **Colón**

Panama Canal

□ **Panama City**

PANAMA

▲ *Barú*
11,468 ft (3,475 m)

• David

Gulf of Panama

• Santiago

miles
0   50

0   50
kilometers

Coffee is a major crop in the cooler tropical highlands of Central America. Crop and livestock farming and forestry are the chief economic activities in Eastern Central America.

NORTHERN CARIBBEAN

The largest Caribbean island nations are Cuba, the Dominican Republic, and Haiti, followed by the Bahamas and Jamaica. Puerto Rico is a US Commonwealth, while the Cayman Islands and the Turks and Caicos Islands are British overseas territories. Most people are descended from Europeans, or Africans who came to the Caribbean as slaves. Sugar and coffee are leading crops. Manufacturing, mining, and tourism are also important.

Fidel Castro led revolutionary forces to power in Cuba in 1959. His Communist policies and his close ties with the former Soviet Union were opposed by the United States.

BAHAMAS

Area: 13,935 sq km (5,380 sq miles)
Population: 284,000
Capital: Nassau (pop. 172,000)
Currency: Bahamian dollar

CUBA

Area: 110,861 sq km (42,804 sq miles)
Population: 11,019,000
Capital: Havana (pop.2,096,000)
Currency: Cuban peso

DOMINICAN REPUBLIC

Area: 48,734 sq km (18,816 sq miles)
Population: 7,964,000
Capital: Santo Domingo (pop. 1,601,000)
Currency: Dominican peso

HAITI

Area: 27,750 sq km (10,714 sq miles)
Population: 7,336,000
Capital: Port-au-Prince (pop.1,144,000)
Currency: Gourde

JAMAICA

Area: 10,991 sq km (4,244 sq miles)
Population: 2,547,000
Capital: Kingston (pop. 588,000)
Currency: Jamaican dollar

OVERSEAS TERRITORIES

CAYMAN ISLANDS (UK)
Area: 259 sq km (100 sq miles)
Population: 32,000
Capital: George Town

PUERTO RICO (US)
Area: 8,897 sq km (3,435 sq miles)
Population: 3,783,000
Capital: San Juan

TURKS AND CAICOS ISLANDS (UK)
Area: 430 sq km (166 sq miles)
Population: 15,000
Capital: Cockburn Town

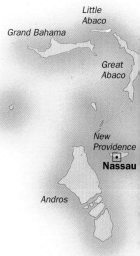

Little Abaco
Grand Bahama
Great Abaco
New Providence
Nassau
Andros

B A H A M A S

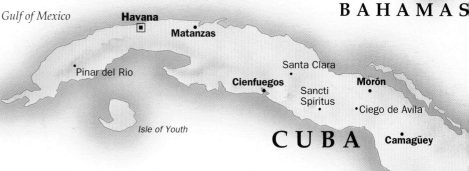

Gulf of Mexico
Havana
Matanzas
Pinar del Rio
Santa Clara
Cienfuegos
Sancti Spiritus
Morón
Ciego de Avila
Isle of Youth
C U B A
Camagüey
Bayamo

George Town
C A Y M A N I S L A N D S (UK)

Montego Bay
Kingston
Spanish Town
J A M A I C A

Caribbean Sea

Cricket is a major sport in Jamaica. It was introduced by the British, who ruled the island for about 300 years until it became independent in 1962. The official language in Jamaica is English.

Sugarcane is grown on many Caribbean islands and it is Cuba's leading export. The islands also produce minerals, including nickel (Cuba), iron and nickel (Dominican Republic), and bauxite (Jamaica).

Banking and other financial services are important in the Bahamas. Many foreign firms and banks have branches there. The islands have no direct taxes, and so many people invest money in the banks.

Tourism is a major activity in the Caribbean. Swimming and snorkelling in the sparkling, sunlit water around the islands in the Bahamas are popular sports. More than 1.5 million tourists visit the Bahamas every year.

San Juan is the capital and largest city of Puerto Rico, a self-governing commonwealth in association with the United States. The chief jobs of the people are in manufacturing, trade, and government.

Roman Catholicism was introduced to Cuba and the Dominican Republic by Spain, and to Haiti by France. Protestantism is important in Jamaica and the Bahamas, which were influenced by Britain.

Eleuthera

Cat

San Salvador

Rum Cay

Great Exuma

Long

Crooked

Mayaguana

Acklins

Great Inagua

Cockburn Town

TURKS AND CAICOS ISLANDS (UK)

Holguin

Guantánamo

Santiago de Cuba

ATLANTIC OCEAN

Cap-Haïtien

Santiago

San Francisco

Gonaives

HAITI

DOMINICAN REPUBLIC

La Romana

Port-au-Prince

Santo Domingo

PUERTO RICO (US)

San Juan

Les Cayes

Jacmel

Ponce

0   100 miles
0   100 kilometers

EASTERN CARIBBEAN

The eastern Caribbean consists mostly of small islands. Some are volcanic, while others are made of coral and limestone. The region contains eight independent countries and eight territories linked to France, the Netherlands, the United States, and Great Britain. Farming and tourism are the chief activities, though Trinidad and Tobago has oil and natural gas. Native Americans once lived on the islands, but people of African descent now form the majority.

Dolphins of several species live in the waters of the Caribbean Sea. Tourists on cruise ships enjoy watching the dolphins. Fishing is an important industry, but nearly all of the catch is sold in local markets,

Road Town

Charlotte Amalie
VIRGIN ISLANDS

(US)

Tourism is a major industry in the eastern Caribbean.The islands are scenically beautiful and have many attractive, sun-baked beaches. Many people visit the islands on cruise ships.

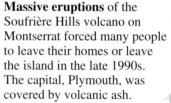

Coconut

Sugarcane

Mace

Cloves

Nutmeg

Cinnamon

Spices, such as cinnamon and nutmeg, are grown on some of the islands in the eastern Caribbean. The main products of the islands include bananas, coconuts, cotton, and sugar.

Massive eruptions of the Soufrière Hills volcano on Montserrat forced many people to leave their homes or leave the island in the late 1990s. The capital, Plymouth, was covered by volcanic ash.

ARUBA(Neth)   **NETHERLANDS ANTILLES**

Aruba   *Curaçao*   *Bonaire*

Willemstad

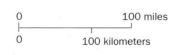

0   100 miles

0   100 kilometers

S O U T H   A M E R I C A

Sailing and fishing are popular tourist activities in the blue waters of the Eastern Caribbean. Local people enjoy a variety of sports, including basketball, cricket, and soccer.

ANGUILLA (UK)
The Valley

ATLANTIC OCEAN

ST KITTS AND NEVIS
Basseterre

ANTIGUA AND BARBUDA
Saint John's

MONTSERRAT (UK)
Plymouth

GUADELOUPE (Fr)
Basse-Terre

DOMINICA
Roseau

MARTINIQUE (Fr)
Fort-de-France

Caribbean Sea

ST LUCIA
Castries

ST VINCENT AND THE GRENADINES
Kingstown

GRENADA
Saint George's

Tobago

TRINIDAD AND TOBAGO
Port of Spain
Trinidad

OVERSEAS TERRITORIES

ANGUILLA (UK)
Area: 96 sq km (37 sq miles)
Population: 8,000
Capital: The Valley

ARUBA (NETHERLANDS)
Area: 75 sq km (29 sq miles)
Population: 77,000
Capital: Oranjestad

GUADELOUPE (FRANCE)
Area: 1,705 sq km (658 sq miles)
Population: 422,000
Capital: Basse-Terre

MARTINIQUE (FRANCE)
Area: 1,102 sq km (425 sq miles)
Population: 384,000
Capital: Fort-de-France

Bridgetown

BARBADOS

MONTSERRAT (UK)
Area: 102 sq km (39 sq miles)
Population: 11,000
Capital: Plymouth

NETHERLANDS ANTILLES
Area: 800 sq km (309 sq miles)
Population: 202,000
Capital: Willemstad

VIRGIN ISLANDS (US)
Area: 340 sq km (131 sq miles)
Population: 98,000
Capital: Charlotte Amalie

VIRGIN ISLANDS (UK)
Area: 153 sq km (59 sq miles)
Population: 20,000
Capital: Road Town

ANTIGUA AND BARBUDA

Area: 440 sq km (170 sq miles)
Population: 66,000
Capital: Saint John s (pop. 38,000)
Currency: East Caribbean dollar

BARBADOS

Area: 431 sq km (166 sq miles)
Population: 264,000
Capital: Bridgetown (pop. 8,000)
Currency: Barbados dollar

DOMINICA

Area: 751 sq km (290 sq miles)
Population: 74,000
Capital: Roseau (pop. 21,000)
Currency: East Caribbean dollar

GRENADA

Area: 344 sq km (133 sq miles)
Population: 99,000
Capital: St. George s (pop. 7,000)
Currency: East Caribbean dollar

ST KITTS AND NEVIS

Area: 261 sq km (101 sq miles)
Population: 41,000
Capital: Basseterre (pop. 15,000)
Currency: East Caribbean dollar

ST LUCIA

Area: 616 sq km (238 sq miles)
Population: 158,000
Capital: Castries (pop. 54,000)
Currency: East Caribbean dollar

ST VINCENT AND THE GRENADINES

Area: 388 sq km (150 sq miles)
Population: 112,000
Capital: Kingstown (pop. 27,000)
Currency: East Caribbean dollar

TRINIDAD AND TOBAGO

Area: 5,130 sq km (1,981 sq miles)
Population: 1,297,000
Capital: Port-of-Spain (pop. 46,000)
Currency: Trinidad & Tobago dollar

PEOPLE AND BELIEFS

North America contains eight percent of the world's population. Vast areas, including most of Canada and Alaska and the deserts of the southwestern United States and northern Mexico, are almost empty of people. Thickly populated areas, with many huge cities, occur in the eastern United States, California, the Mexican plateau, Central America, and the Caribbean.

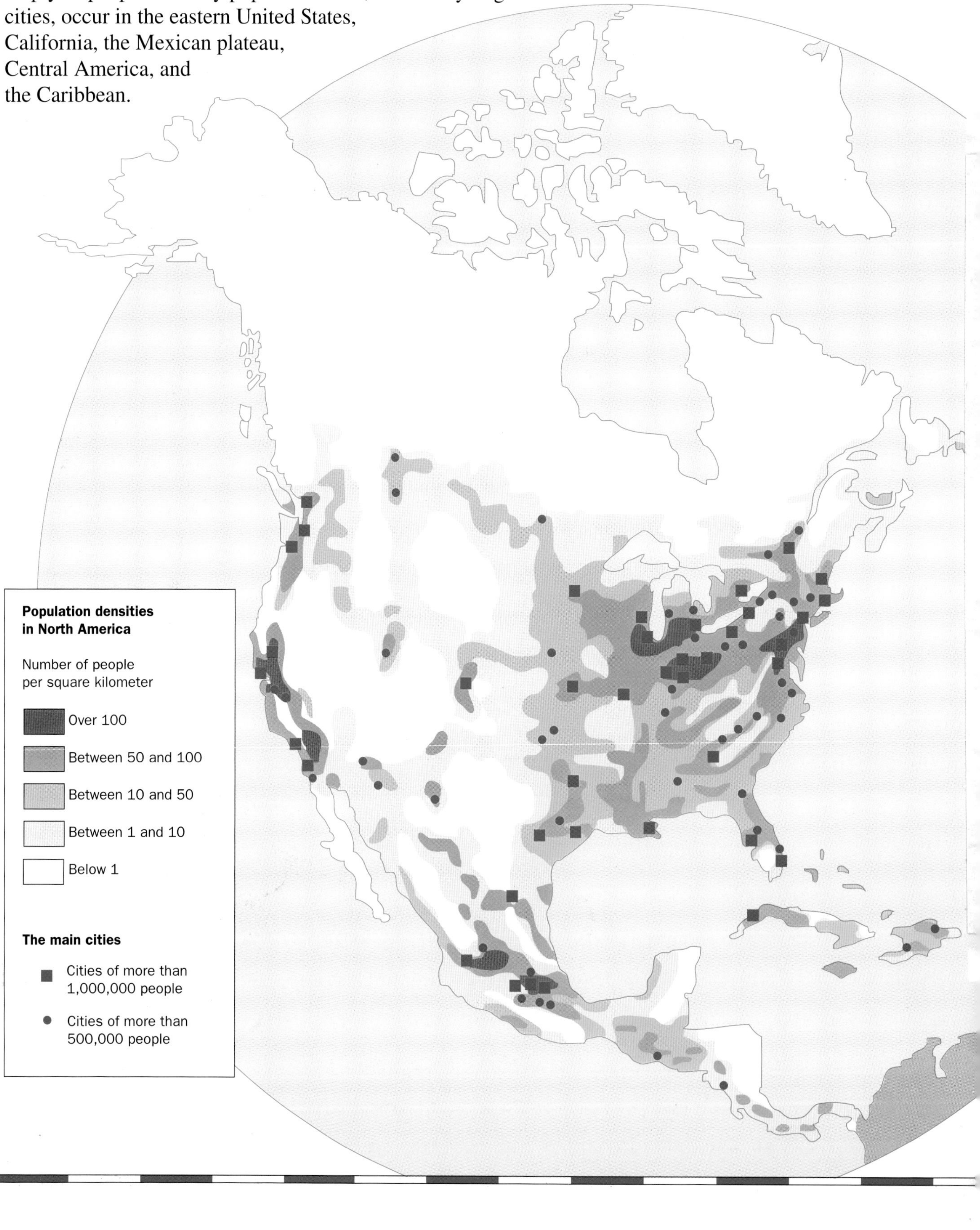

Population densities in North America

Number of people per square kilometer

Over 100

Between 50 and 100

Between 10 and 50

Between 1 and 10

Below 1

The main cities

■ Cities of more than 1,000,000 people

● Cities of more than 500,000 people

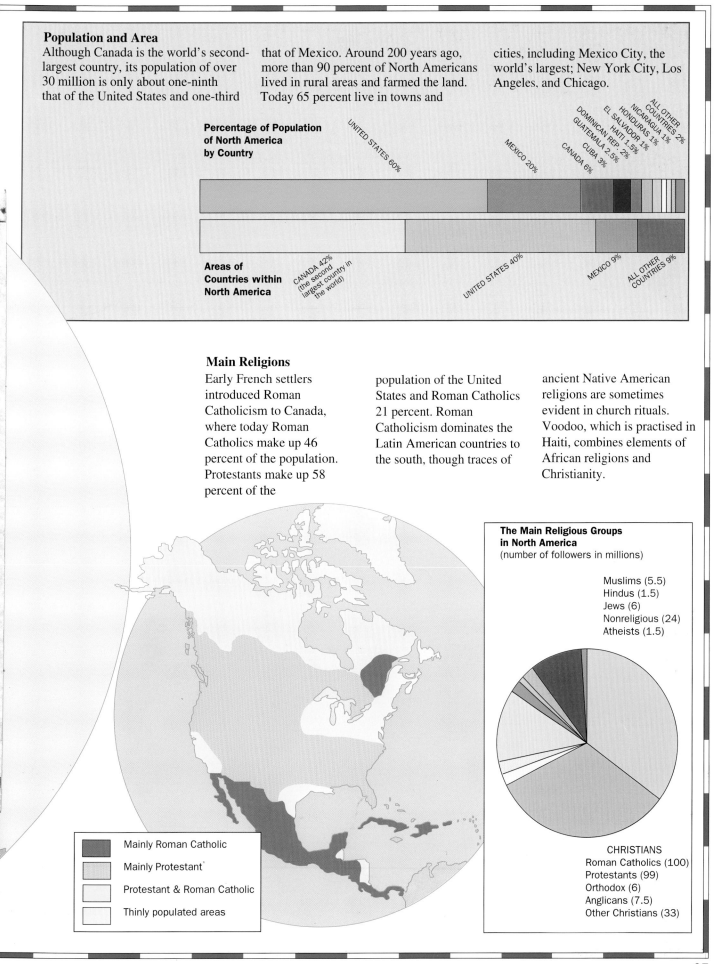

Population and Area

Although Canada is the world's second-largest country, its population of over 30 million is only about one-ninth that of the United States and one-third that of Mexico. Around 200 years ago, more than 90 percent of North Americans lived in rural areas and farmed the land. Today 65 percent live in towns and cities, including Mexico City, the world's largest; New York City, Los Angeles, and Chicago.

Percentage of Population of North America by Country

UNITED STATES 60%
MEXICO 20%
CANADA 6%
CUBA 3%
GUATEMALA 2.5%
DOMINICAN REP. 2%
HAITI 1.5%
EL SALVADOR 1.5%
HONDURAS 1%
NICARAGUA 1%
ALL OTHER COUNTRIES 2%

Areas of Countries within North America

CANADA 42% (the second largest country in the world)
UNITED STATES 40%
MEXICO 9%
ALL OTHER COUNTRIES 9%

Main Religions

Early French settlers introduced Roman Catholicism to Canada, where today Roman Catholics make up 46 percent of the population. Protestants make up 58 percent of the population of the United States and Roman Catholics 21 percent. Roman Catholicism dominates the Latin American countries to the south, though traces of ancient Native American religions are sometimes evident in church rituals. Voodoo, which is practised in Haiti, combines elements of African religions and Christianity.

Mainly Roman Catholic
Mainly Protestant
Protestant & Roman Catholic
Thinly populated areas

The Main Religious Groups in North America
(number of followers in millions)

Muslims (5.5)
Hindus (1.5)
Jews (6)
Nonreligious (24)
Atheists (1.5)

CHRISTIANS
Roman Catholics (100)
Protestants (99)
Orthodox (6)
Anglicans (7.5)
Other Christians (33)

CLIMATE AND VEGETATION

North America has every kind of climatic and vegetation region. The north is cold, but the United States has large areas of temperate forest and grasslands. Deserts cover parts of the southwestern United States, while southern Mexico, the Caribbean, and Central America lie in the hot tropics.

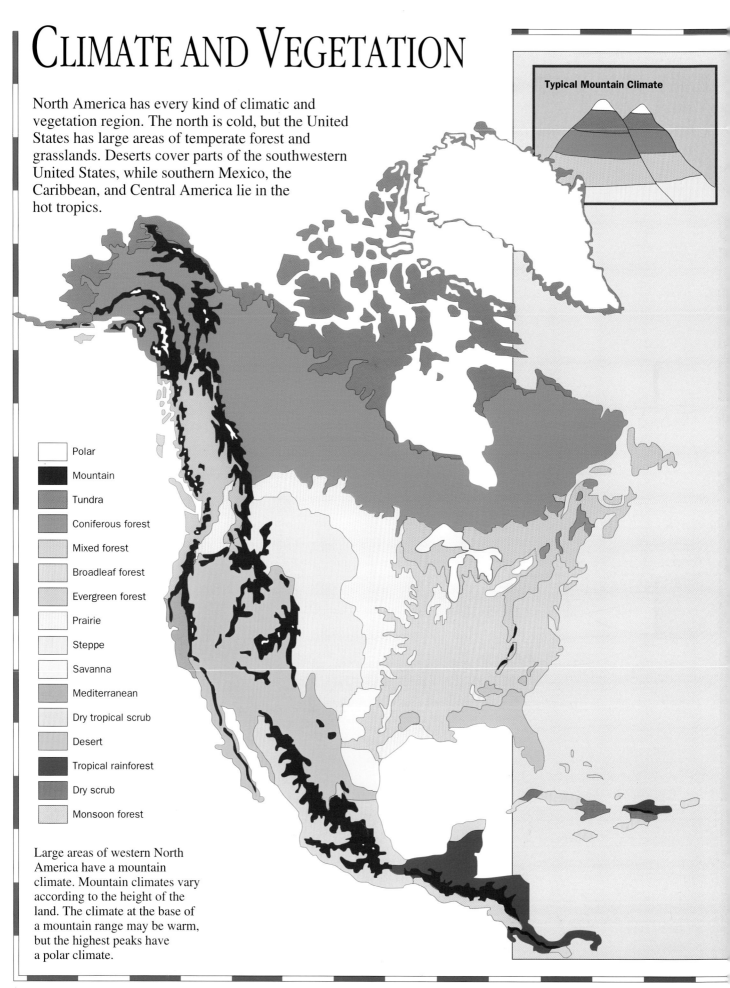

Typical Mountain Climate

Polar

Mountain

Tundra

Coniferous forest

Mixed forest

Broadleaf forest

Evergreen forest

Prairie

Steppe

Savanna

Mediterranean

Dry tropical scrub

Desert

Tropical rainforest

Dry scrub

Monsoon forest

Large areas of western North America have a mountain climate. Mountain climates vary according to the height of the land. The climate at the base of a mountain range may be warm, but the highest peaks have a polar climate.

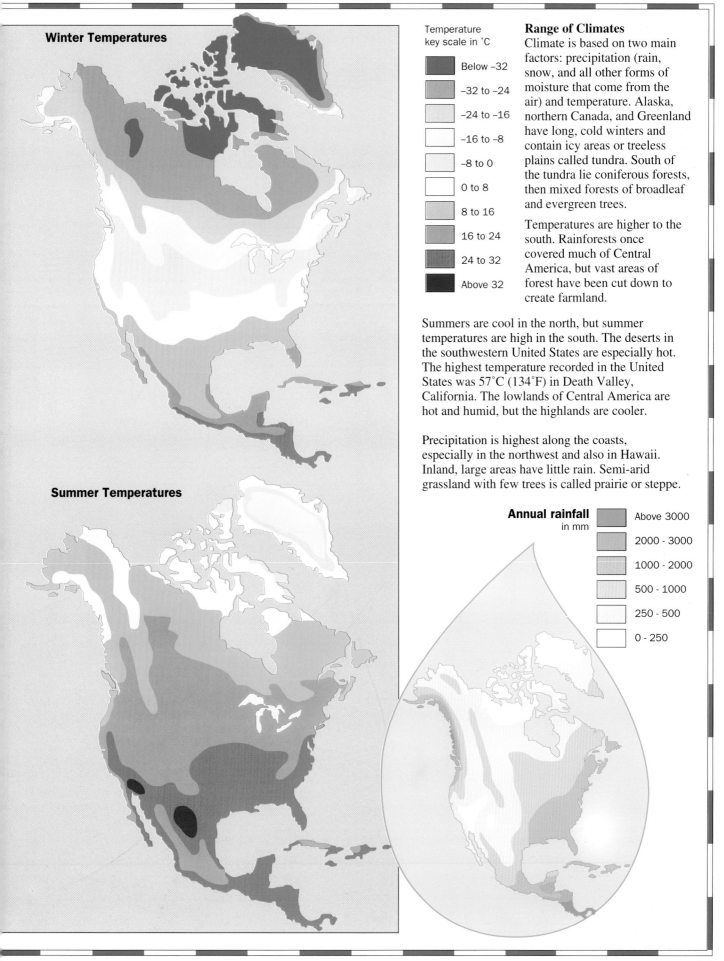

Winter Temperatures

Summer Temperatures

Temperature
key scale in °C

	Below –32
	–32 to –24
	–24 to –16
	–16 to –8
	–8 to 0
	0 to 8
	8 to 16
	16 to 24
	24 to 32
	Above 32

Range of Climates

Climate is based on two main factors: precipitation (rain, snow, and all other forms of moisture that come from the air) and temperature. Alaska, northern Canada, and Greenland have long, cold winters and contain icy areas or treeless plains called tundra. South of the tundra lie coniferous forests, then mixed forests of broadleaf and evergreen trees.

Temperatures are higher to the south. Rainforests once covered much of Central America, but vast areas of forest have been cut down to create farmland.

Summers are cool in the north, but summer temperatures are high in the south. The deserts in the southwestern United States are especially hot. The highest temperature recorded in the United States was 57°C (134°F) in Death Valley, California. The lowlands of Central America are hot and humid, but the highlands are cooler.

Precipitation is highest along the coasts, especially in the northwest and also in Hawaii. Inland, large areas have little rain. Semi-arid grassland with few trees is called prairie or steppe.

Annual rainfall
in mm

	Above 3000
	2000 - 3000
	1000 - 2000
	500 - 1000
	250 - 500
	0 - 250

ECOLOGY AND ENVIRONMENT

The land is always changing. Natural forces, such as volcanic eruptions, great storms, and unceasing erosion contribute to the change. People also change the land. Human activities cause pollution, while intensive farming exposes the land to the wind and rain, turning former grasslands into desert.

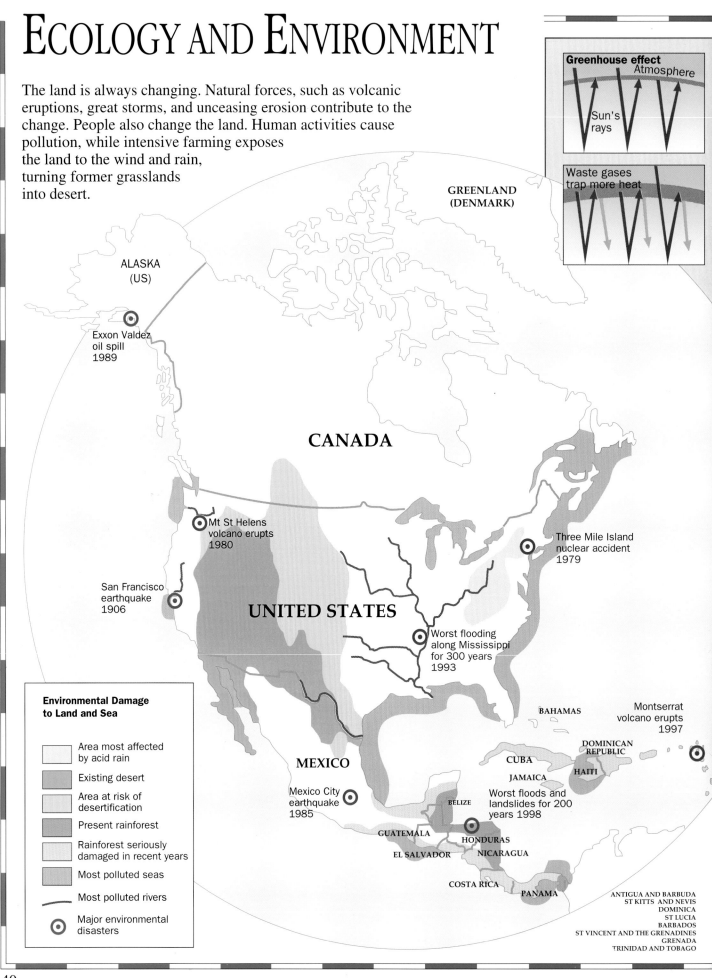

Greenhouse effect
Atmosphere
Sun's rays

Waste gases trap more heat

GREENLAND
(DENMARK)

ALASKA
(US)

Exxon Valdez
oil spill
1989

CANADA

Mt St Helens
volcano erupts
1980

Three Mile Island
nuclear accident
1979

San Francisco
earthquake
1906

UNITED STATES

Worst flooding
along Mississippi
for 300 years
1993

BAHAMAS

Montserrat
volcano erupts
1997

DOMINICAN
REPUBLIC

CUBA

MEXICO

JAMAICA

HAITI

Mexico City
earthquake
1985

BELIZE

Worst floods and
landslides for 200
years 1998

GUATEMALA

HONDURAS

EL SALVADOR

NICARAGUA

COSTA RICA

PANAMA

ANTIGUA AND BARBUDA
ST KITTS AND NEVIS
DOMINICA
ST LUCIA
BARBADOS
ST VINCENT AND THE GRENADINES
GRENADA
TRINIDAD AND TOBAGO

Environmental Damage to Land and Sea

Area most affected by acid rain

Existing desert

Area at risk of desertification

Present rainforest

Rainforest seriously damaged in recent years

Most polluted seas

Most polluted rivers

Major environmental disasters

Damaging the Environment

Air pollution is a problem in North America, where factories, cars, and homes emit waste gases into the air. Some gases dissolve in water vapor and cause acid rain, which kills trees. Excess cabon dioxide increases the atmosphere's natural greenhouse effect and may be causing global warming.

The clearing of forests and of grasslands lays soil bare. Strong winds and rain remove the topsoil, making the land barren. The destruction of rainforests also threatens many living creatures with extinction.

Water pollution is caused by agricultural chemicals and waste from factories being washed or pumped into rivers and lakes, and by oil spills and untreated sewage at sea. Pollution is also caused by accidents at nuclear power stations. Today, people are working to combat pollution and its deadly effects.

Natural Hazards

Earthquakes are common in western North America and the Caribbean, which lie on unstable parts of the earth's crust. Volcanic eruptions occur in Alaska, Washington, Mexico, Central America and the Caribbean. Hurricanes cause great damage in the Caribbean and the southeastern United States, while violent tornadoes tear through the central plains of the United States. Devastating floods occur when rivers overflow.

Natural Hazards

 Earthquake zones

 Active volcanoes

 Hurricane tracks (June to October)

 Tornado danger areas

Endangered Species

North America was once a vast, mostly empty wilderness, where many wild animals flourished. But in the last 400 years, hunting and the destruction of natural vegetation have greatly reduced the numbers of animals. Some species are close to extinction.

Fortunately, many endangered species are now protected, and some have begun to recover their numbers. Even the bald eagle, symbol of the United States, was threatened, but the US government announced in 1999 that its numbers had recovered sufficiently for it to be removed from the endangered list after 32 years.

California condor

Some Endangered Species of North America

Birds
California condor
Eskimo curlew
Ivory-billed woodpecker
Prairie chicken

Mammals
American bison
Black bear
Central American tapir
Jaguarundi
Volcano rabbit

Marine mammals
Grey whale
Manatee

Trees
Caribbean mahogany
Giant sequoia

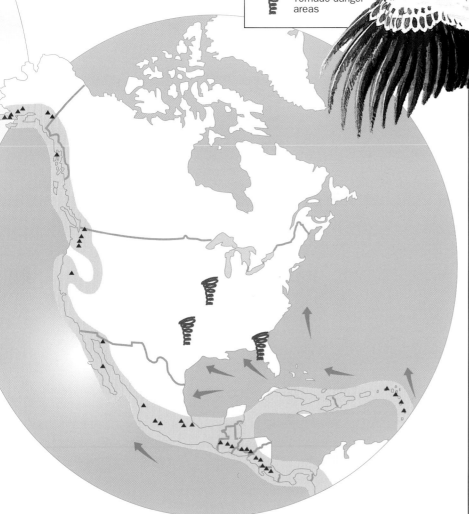

Economy

North America is rich in natural resources, including coal, oil, gas, and most of the metals used in industry. It also has forests and large areas of fertile farmland. The most developed countries are the United States and Canada. Together, they produce about one-third of the world's industrial goods.

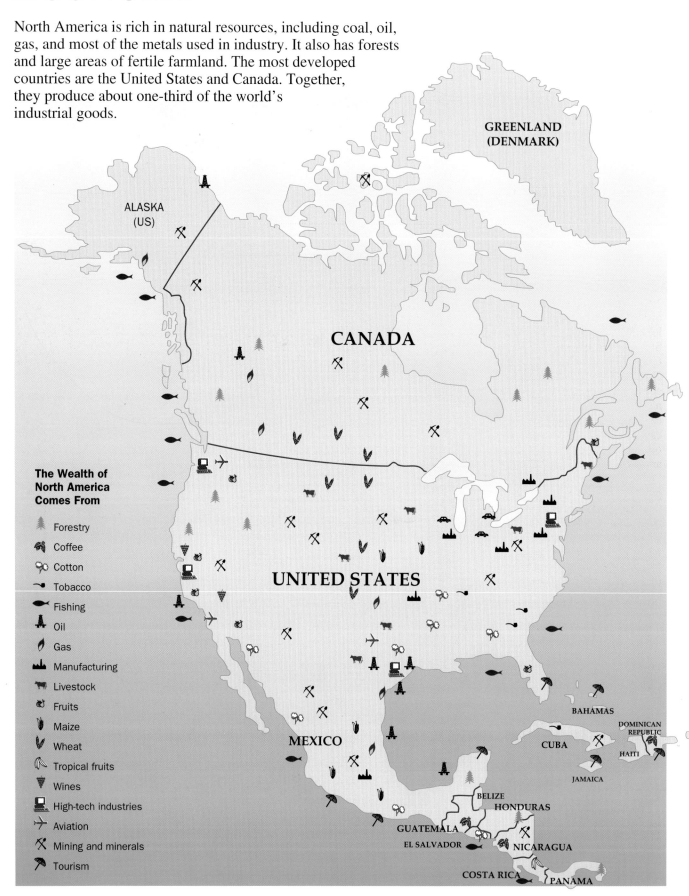

GREENLAND
(DENMARK)

ALASKA
(US)

CANADA

**The Wealth of
North America
Comes From**

🌲 Forestry

🍇 Coffee

🌿 Cotton

🌿 Tobacco

🐟 Fishing

🛢 Oil

🔥 Gas

🏭 Manufacturing

🐄 Livestock

🍒 Fruits

🌽 Maize

🌾 Wheat

🍌 Tropical fruits

🍇 Wines

💻 High-tech industries

✈ Aviation

⛏ Mining and minerals

☂ Tourism

UNITED STATES

MEXICO

BAHAMAS

CUBA

HAITI

DOMINICAN
REPUBLIC

JAMAICA

BELIZE

HONDURAS

GUATEMALA

EL SALVADOR

NICARAGUA

COSTA RICA

PANAMA

Gross National Product

In order to compare the economies of countries, experts work out the gross national product (GNP) of the countries in US dollars. The GNP, is the total value of all the goods and services produced in a country in a year. The pie chart, right, shows that the GNP of the United States is more than seven times bigger than the combined GNPs of all the other countries in North America. No other country in the world has a higher GNP than the United States.

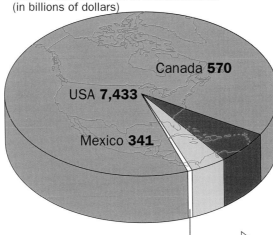

GNP for the Countries of North America
(in billions of dollars)

Canada **570**

USA **7,433**

Mexico **341**

All other countries

Cuba **17**
Guatemala **16**
Dominican Republic **12**
El Salvador **10**
Costa Rica **9**
Panama **8**
Trinidad and Tobago **5**
Honduras **4**
Jamaica **4**
Bahamas **3**
Barbados **2**
Haiti **2**
Nicaragua **2**
Belize **0.6**
Antigua & Barbuda **0.5**
St Lucia **0.5**
Grenada **0.3**
Dominica **0.2**
St Kitts and Nevis **0.2**
St Vincent & Grenadines **0.2**

Per Capita GNPs

Per capita means per head or per person. Per capita GNPs are worked out by dividing the GNP by the population. For example, the per capita GNP of the United States is $28,020. Canada has a per capita GNP of $19,020. Poor countries have low per capita GNPs. For example, Haiti has a per capita GNP of only $310.

Sources of Energy

North America produces about one-fifth of the world's oil. The leading producer is the United States, followed by Mexico, Canada, Trinidad, and Tobago. North America also produces about one-third of the world's natural gas. Hydroelectricity (water power) is important, especially in Canada, while other important energy sources are coal and uranium.

In the United States, oil provides about 39 percent of the total energy produced, natural gas about 24 and coal 22 percent. Other sources of energy, including hydroelectric and nuclear plants, account for around 15 percent.

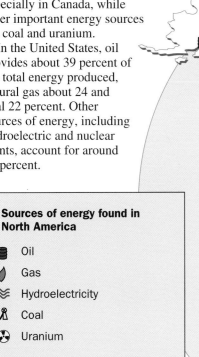

Sources of energy found in North America

- 🛢 Oil
- 💧 Gas
- ≋ Hydroelectricity
- ⚒ Coal
- ☢ Uranium

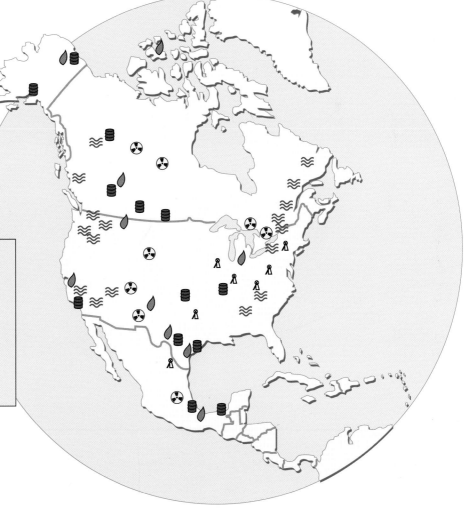

ANTIGUA AND BARBUDA
ST KITTS AND NEVIS
DOMINICA
ST LUCIA
BARBADOS
ST VINCENT AND THE GRENADINES
GRENADA
TRINIDAD AND TOBAGO

POLITICS AND HISTORY

North America contains 23 independent countries. The United States and Mexico are federal republics. Canada, Belize, and eight Caribbean nations are constitutional monarchies. They have their own governments, but they recognize the British monarch as their head of state. Ten countries are democratic republics. while Cuba is a Communist republic. North America also includes 14 overseas territories linked to Britain, Denmark, France, Netherlands, and the United States.

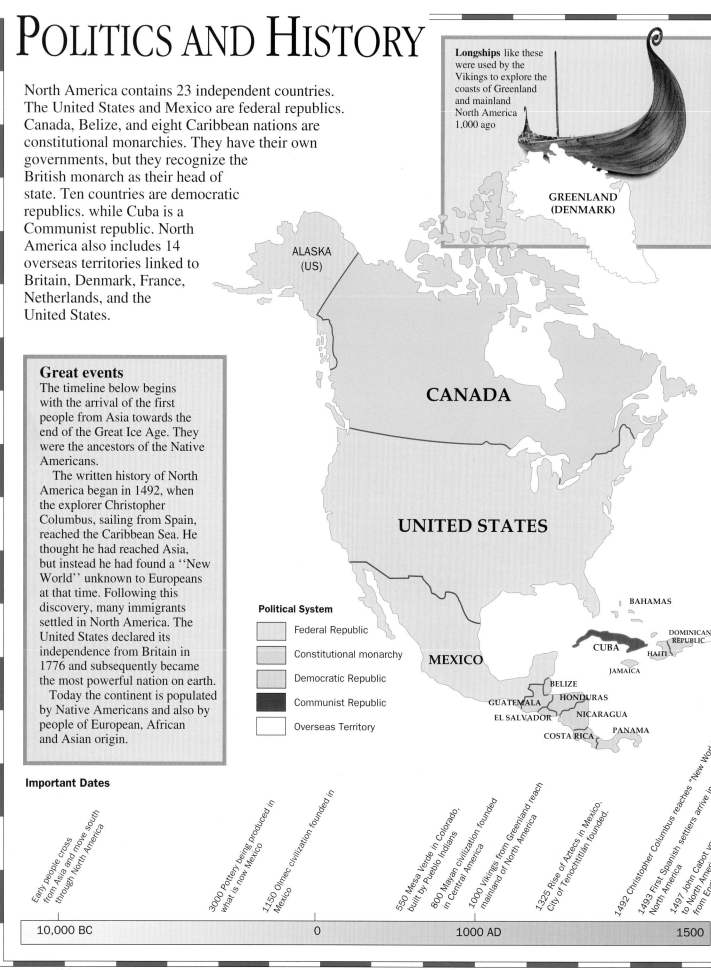

Longships like these were used by the Vikings to explore the coasts of Greenland and mainland North America 1,000 ago

GREENLAND (DENMARK)

ALASKA (US)

CANADA

UNITED STATES

MEXICO

BAHAMAS

CUBA

DOMINICAN REPUBLIC

HAITI

JAMAICA

BELIZE
GUATEMALA
HONDURAS
EL SALVADOR
NICARAGUA
COSTA RICA
PANAMA

Great events

The timeline below begins with the arrival of the first people from Asia towards the end of the Great Ice Age. They were the ancestors of the Native Americans.

The written history of North America began in 1492, when the explorer Christopher Columbus, sailing from Spain, reached the Caribbean Sea. He thought he had reached Asia, but instead he had found a ''New World'' unknown to Europeans at that time. Following this discovery, many immigrants settled in North America. The United States declared its independence from Britain in 1776 and subsequently became the most powerful nation on earth.

Today the continent is populated by Native Americans and also by people of European, African and Asian origin.

Political System

- Federal Republic
- Constitutional monarchy
- Democratic Republic
- Communist Republic
- Overseas Territory

Important Dates

Early people cross from Asia and move south through North America

3000 Pottery being produced in what is now Mexico

1150 Olmec civilization founded in Mexico

550 Mesa Verde in Colorado, built by Pueblo Indians

800 Mayan civilization founded in Central America

1000 Vikings from Greenland reach mainland of North America

1325 Rise of Aztecs in Mexico. City of Tenochtitlán founded.

1492 Christopher Columbus reaches "New World"

1493 First Spanish settlers arrive in North America

1497 John Cabot voy to North Americ from Engl

| 10,000 BC | 0 | 1000 AD | 1500 |

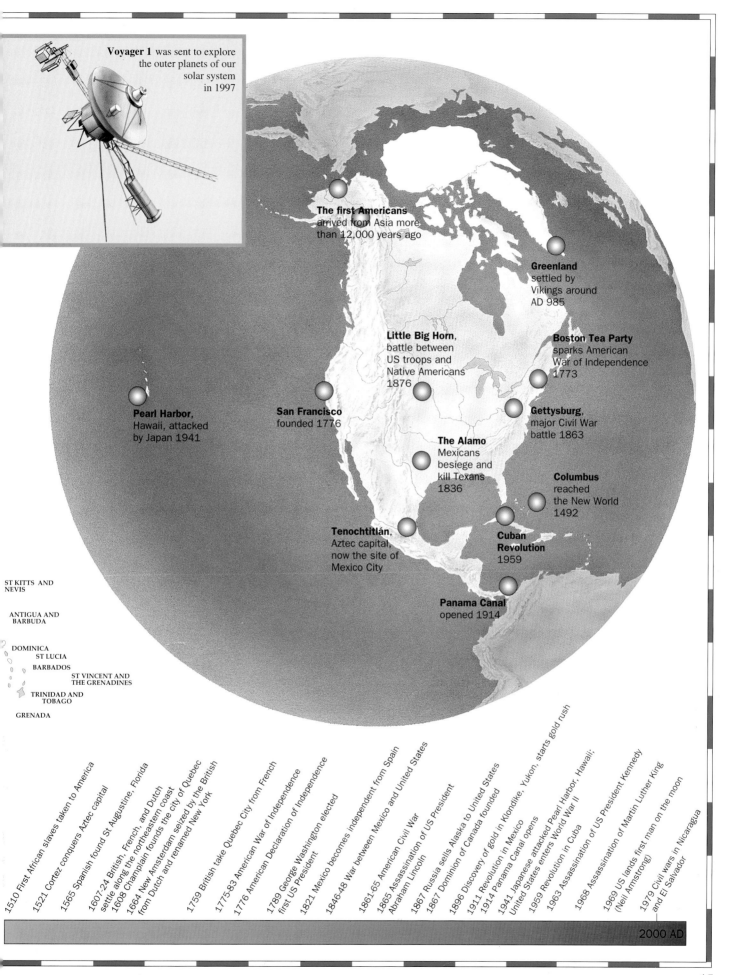

Voyager 1 was sent to explore the outer planets of our solar system in 1997

The first Americans arrived from Asia more than 12,000 years ago

Greenland settled by Vikings around AD 985

Little Big Horn, battle between US troops and Native Americans 1876

Boston Tea Party sparks American War of Independence 1773

Pearl Harbor, Hawaii, attacked by Japan 1941

San Francisco founded 1776

Gettysburg, major Civil War battle 1863

The Alamo Mexicans besiege and kill Texans 1836

Columbus reached the New World 1492

Tenochtitlán, Aztec capital, now the site of Mexico City

Cuban Revolution 1959

Panama Canal opened 1914

ST KITTS AND NEVIS

ANTIGUA AND BARBUDA

DOMINICA
ST LUCIA
BARBADOS
ST VINCENT AND THE GRENADINES
TRINIDAD AND TOBAGO

GRENADA

1510 First African slaves taken to America

1521 Cortez conquers Aztec capital

1565 Spanish found St Augustine, Florida

1607-24 British, French and Dutch settle along the northeastern coast

1608 Champlain founds the city of Quebec

1664 New Amsterdam seized by the British from Dutch and renamed New York

1759 British take Quebec City from French

1775-83 American War of Independence

1776 American Declaration of Independence

1789 George Washington elected first US President

1821 Mexico becomes independent from Spain

1846-48 War between Mexico and United States

1861-65 American Civil War

1865 Assassination of US President Abraham Lincoln

1867 Russia sells Alaska to United States

1867 Dominion of Canada founded

1896 Discovery of gold in Klondike, Yukon, starts gold rush

1911 Revolution in Mexico

1914 Panama Canal opens

1941 Japanese attacked Pearl Harbor, Hawaii; United States enters World War II

1959 Revolution in Cuba

1963 Assassination of US President Kennedy

1968 Assassination of Martin Luther King

1969 US lands first man on the moon (Neil Armstrong)

1979 Civil wars in Nicaragua and El Salvador

2000 AD

INDEX

Numbers in **bold** are map references
Numbers in *italics* are picture references

Picture credits
Photographs: Travel Photo International 1, 5, 9, 13, 21, 23, 25, 26, 27, 33, 34
AS Publishing 4, 10, 15
Keith Lye 4, 29